DIAMOND
HANDBOOK

Joseph Asscher cleaving the famous Cullinan diamond, which at 3,105 carats was the world's largest diamond (February 10th, 1908). It was found in the Premier Mine in South Africa and cut into nine principal diamonds. Cullinan I, the largest diamond, is mounted in the British Royal Sceptre and weighs 530.20 carats. *Photo from the Royal Asscher Diamond Company.*

DIAMOND
HANDBOOK
How to Look at Diamonds & Avoid Ripoffs

Renée Newman

International Jewelry Publications
Los Angeles

International Jewelry Publications
P.O. Box 13384
Los Angeles, CA 90013-0384 USA

(Inquiries should be accompanied by a self-addressed, stamped envelope.)

Printed in Singapore

Library of Congress Cataloging-in-Publication Data

Newman, Renée.
    Diamond handbook : how to look at diamonds & avoid ripoffs / Renée
    Newman.
        p. cm.
    Includes bibliographical references and index.
    ISBN 0-929975-36-7 (trade paperback : alk. paper)
        1. Diamonds–Purchasing–Handbooks; manuals, etc. I. Title

TS753.N44 2005
736'.23–dc22
                                                                    2004056994

Cover photo:
A modern cushion-cut diamond solitaire with pear-shaped side diamonds set in platinum, approximately 20-carats total weight. Ring and photo from Harry Winston, Inc.

Title page photo:
Royal Brilliant® diamond. Stone and photo from Exroyal Co. Inc.

Contents

Acknowledgments

I would like to express my appreciation to the following people and companies for their contribution to the *Diamond Handbook*:

Ernie and Regina Goldberger of the Josam Diamond Trading Corporation. This book could never have been written without the experience and knowledge I gained from working with them. A large percentage of the loose diamonds pictured in this book are or were part of their collection.

Eve Alfillé, C.R. Beesley, Charles Carmona, Paul Cassarino, Adam Daniels, Branko Deljanin, Doug & Beth, Jerry Ehrenwald, Michael Goldstein, Alan Hodgkinson, Mickey Ishida, Wolf Kuehn, Gail Levine, Lynn Ramsey, Barry Rogoff, Howard Rubin, Debra Sawatsky, Michael Schachter, Sindi Schloss, Steve & Mary, Tom Tashey, Jennifer Thornton Davis, John S. White, Sharrie Woodring, Peter Yantzer, Gary Zimmerman. They have made valuable suggestions, corrections and comments regarding the portions of the book they examined. They are not responsible for any possible errors, nor do they necessarily endorse the material contained in this book.

The teachers at the GIA. They helped me obtain the technical background needed to write a book such as this.

Ebert & Co., Mark Gronlund, J. Landau, Inc., and D & E Singer. Their stones or jewelry have been used for some of the photographs.

Baroka Creations, Bez Ambar Diamonds, Inc., Britestar Diamond Co., Paul Cassarino, Dali Diamond Co., Diamco, Joseph Dumouchelle International Auctioneers, Exroyal Co., Gem International, Gemological Institute of America, William Goldberg Corp, Yuval Harary Diamonds, Alan Hodgkinson, HRD, Doron Isaac, Scott Keating, J. Landau, Inc., Lili Diamonds, Gail Levine, Douglas Mays, National Diamond Syndicate, Royal Asscher Diamond Co., Mark Silverstein, Ernest Slotar, Inc., Suberi Bros, Trillion Diamond Co, Tycoon Jewelry, Harry Winston, Inc., and Robert Weldon. Photos and/or diagrams from them have been reproduced in this book.

Don Nelson and Joyce Ng. They have provided technical assistance.

Louise Harris Berlin. She has spent hours carefully editing the *Diamond Handbook*. Thanks to her, this book is much easier for consumers to read and understand.

My sincere thanks to all of these contributors for their kindness and help.

Preface

When my first book, the *Diamond Ring Buying Guide,* was published in 1989, it was designed to be a basic guide to evaluating diamonds and ring mountings. Over the years I've updated it and added a lot of color photos and new information. However, in order to maintain a competitive price, it's no longer possible to increase the number of pages.

Readers have requested information on diamond grading reports, appraisals, antique jewelry, recutting, and branded diamonds— topics not included in the *Diamond Ring Buying Guide*. They also want me to expand on subjects that I've already covered, such as fluorescence, synthetic diamonds, and fancy shapes. The logical solution was to write a new book on diamonds, which I've entitled the *Diamond Handbook*. Details on judging diamond quality are also included in this new book, but they are presented differently with new photos.

One of the biggest differences in the *Diamond Handbook* is that it's in black and white, which enables it to have a higher page count than the full color Diamond Ring Buying Guide, yet still remain affordable. There's another advantage to black and white photography; it's easier to compare shape, cut, and clarity because the color of all the diamonds is the same. The variations of color in diamond photographs can sometimes be distracting.

The *Diamond Handbook* is designed to be a complement to the *Diamond Ring Buying Guide*, not a substitute. If you are looking for information on gold, platinum, settings styles, ring mountings, diamond care, and detecting diamond imitations, you should purchase the *Diamond Ring Buying Guide*. It also has more information on treatments, carat weight and fancy color diamonds.

Both books share a common goal—to help you visually evaluate diamonds. Grading reports don't tell you everything you should know about a diamond, and they are too expensive to be a worthwhile option when purchasing small diamonds. Therefore to be a savvy buyer, you should learn how to look at diamonds and make judgments about their quality. If you're able to do this, you will not only be able to get better buys, you'll also have a greater appreciation for the diamonds you select.

1

How to Look at Diamonds

A relative (let's call her Sally) wanted me to get her a pair of ¼ carat diamonds (total weight ½ carat) for stud earrings. Since I used to work full-time in the diamond industry, I have contacts where I can buy diamonds at wholesale.

Sally wanted some decent looking diamonds for as low of a price as possible. She didn't care if the diamonds had several imperfections as long as they were not eye-visible (SI_2–high I_1 clarity range). A dealer I know had a parcel of about 250 near-colorless diamonds in that clarity range, which weighed close to 0.25 carats each.

The dealer allowed me to quickly look through part of the parcel and find diamonds that matched. My goal was to pick out the best possible stones for Sally, but after I had looked at about fifty diamonds with a 10-power loupe and arranged them in little piles according to their quality, the dealer reminded me I was getting a parcel price, not a pick price. (The definition of "parcel price" can vary from one dealer to another. For some dealers, it means the price at which they'll sell you the entire parcel. For other dealers, "parcel price" may mean the price at which they'll sell random stones from the parcel, with no picking allowed. Some other dealers will allow you to pick through some of the stones, but not the entire parcel.)

I rechecked two little piles of potential diamonds with the loupe, picked out the ones I liked, measured their diameters, selected four of about the same diameter, and then checked them face up to see which ones matched the best.

I had to do all this in about fifteen or twenty minutes because the dealer had a lot of other business to take care of and was giving me a parcel price. There was no time to view the diamonds under a microscope.

The fact that I knew how to look at diamonds and choose the ones with the best qualities saved Sally a lot of money. If I had asked the dealer for two SI_2, H or I color diamonds, the prices would have been determined by referring to a "wholesale" price list and subtracting an appropriate discount; and the resulting price would have been higher.

If I'd asked for a lab grading report for each of those diamonds, the diamonds would have cost me about double what I paid. Not only would I have had to pay for the reports, I would have had to pay indirectly for the time required to select the diamonds and send them to the lab. Yet the reports would not have told me as much about the quality of the diamonds as I was able to determine with my eyes. A lab report could have confirmed that the diamonds were genuine, natural, and untreated; but I know the dealer and trust him.

If Sally had wanted a single half-carat diamond for an engagement ring, I would have recommended that she get at least a "mini" diamond grading report for insurance and verification purposes. In addition, I would have been more concerned about the symmetry and polish of the diamond, and I would have spent a lot more time selecting and evaluating the stone because of the greater value and significance of the diamond.

However, whether I'm selecting small diamonds for earrings or a large one for an engagement ring, I care about brilliance, sparkle, and transparency—characteristics, which aren't described on grading reports. I also care about the overall quality of the cut. In Chapters 3 and 4, I explain which cut factors I consider to be most important.

Why Should Consumers Learn How to Look at Diamonds?

I explained above how my ability to visually evaluate diamonds helped me get a better price and better diamonds. If you are a consumer, you may be wondering how this skill can help you since you don't have access to wholesale diamond dealers with parcels of diamonds. You should learn the basics of how to look at diamonds because:

◆ **You will be able to select better diamond semi-mounts, pendants, bracelets, earrings and brooches.** Even though the center stone of a ring will most likely come with a lab report, the other diamonds in the mounting probably won't. You're going to have to determine with your eye, whether the quality of the smaller diamonds is comparable to the quality of the center diamond. What's the point of spending a lot of time and money on selecting a top-quality diamond and then mounting it with diamonds that are obviously low-grade?

Most likely you will be buying other diamond jewelry during your lifetime. If you are able to visually judge differences in the quality of the diamonds, this can help you compare prices and make wise choices. Granted, if you're a consumer, you probably won't be able to see fine differences of clarity and color, but you can learn to tell the difference between a very slightly imperfect diamond and one that's imperfect.

You can also learn to see the difference between a faint yellow diamond and one that's colorless.

◆ **Grading reports don't tell you everything about your diamond.** As mentioned earlier, many diamond certificates don't provide much information about the quality of the cut, and they don't describe the brilliance of the diamond. Even though future lab reports may indicate these qualities, what your eyes see when you wear the diamond is more important than what a machine can measure.

◆ **There's a range of qualities within each clarity grade.** The inclusions (imperfections) in some SI$_2$'s are more obvious than in other SI$_2$'s (stones with a slightly imperfect clarity). If you look at the stones under 10-power magnification instead of relying just on the lab report grade, you can, for example, select a diamond whose imperfections are less noticeable. In some cases, you can also choose the one with the most interesting looking crystal inclusions. Even though lab reports have diagrams of the inclusions, their appearance through a loupe or microscope is quite different.

Another consideration is that color and clarity grades are highly subjective. As a result, the gem trade accepts a tolerance of plus or minus one grade.

◆ **You will be more qualified to evaluate salespeople and jewelers.** If, for example, you're able to spot major differences in the quality of the cut, and a sales person tells you that a poorly cut diamond is well made, you will know that you should find someone more competent to help you select a well-cut diamond.

◆ **You will be able to compare prices more accurately.** Poor cuts may be discounted as much as 40%. Top cuts may carry premiums of 10–15%. Consequently there may be a major difference in price between two diamonds of the same weight, shape, color and clarity if their cut quality is different.

◆ **You will be able to appreciate diamonds more after you purchase them**. How can you appreciate something you don't understand? If you're able to visually compare your diamonds to those with inferior brilliance and sparkle, this will help you realize why yours are special.

◆ **You will have more fun shopping for diamonds.**

What Type of Magnification is Used for Viewing Diamonds?

Diamond dealers typically view diamonds with a 10-power (10X) triplet loupe (fig. 1.1). A triplet loupe has three lenses that are held in place by a metal ring. One lens is the magnifier, one lens corrects color distortions and another corrects linear distortions. The advantages of the loupe are that it is portable, affordable and faster to use than a microscope.

One way to learn how to use a loupe is to ask a jeweler or loupe salesperson to show you how. You can find loupes at jewelry supply stores, rock shops and public gem shows. They normally cost at least $25 if they are of good quality.

Fig. 1.1 A 10-power triplet loupe

At the Tucson 2004 Gem show, a jewelry supply dealer was selling a flat-shape loupe at a price so good that I bought ten of them. The dealer said they were 10-power and they had the markings "triplet 10X" so I assumed the loupes *were* 10-power. When I got home I noticed that inclusions looked unusually small through these loupes. I then compared them to my other loupes and magnifiers and determined that the loupes I had bought were 4-power. The morals of the story are don't always believe what you read; and if a deal seems too good to be true, it probably is. Normally, however, if a loupe resembles the one in figure 1.1 and is marked 10X triplet, it is a 10-power triplet loupe.

Before you use the loupe to look at diamonds, you may wish to try focusing it on your fingernail. You'll have to hold the loupe about ¾ of an inch (a little less than 2 centimeters) from the fingernail. If you hold the loupe close to your eye, you'll have a broader range of view than when you hold it further away from the eye. The distance of your fingernail, however, must remain at the same close distance to the loupe in order for it to remain in focus.

Gemologists and gem laboratories use a microscope for most of the diamond grading process. In his book *Photo Masters for Diamond Grading* (pg.4), Gary Roskn states that gem labs use a higher magnification than 10-power to help speed up the grading process. By starting with higher power, it's easier for lab graders to locate small inclusions. To make the final judgment, the microscope is reduced to 10-power. Afterwards graders view the diamond with a 10-power loupe to decide the final grade.

Dealers and gemologists both use microscopes to help them detect treated diamonds and synthetic diamonds. Microscopes permit them to view diamonds at higher powers with a greater variety of lighting.

What Type of Lighting is Best for Viewing Diamonds?

The GIA states in its Diamond Grading Course that the most accepted lighting for grading the color of diamonds is balanced, daylight-equivalent fluorescent light. According to the GIA, the overhead light on many gemological microscopes provides this kind of light. In most cases, it doesn't matter what type of fluorescent light lay people use to view diamonds because they have to rely on lab reports for exact color grades.

Diamond dealers also use fluorescent lights when evaluating diamond quality. They provide an even, diffused light, which is ideal for judging the brilliance of the diamond. (Diffused light is spread over a wide area instead of concentrated on one spot. Translucent white plastic can diffuse the concentrated light of a clear light bulb or halogen spotlight.)

Halogen spotlights, incandescent light bulbs, and candlelight can often highlight a diamond's sparkle (technically called **scintillation**) and fire (spectral colors). They may also make diamonds appear a bit more yellowish than they would look in daylight or under a fluorescent light. As a result, these light sources are not recommended for diamond grading.

When the GIA gem trade lab grades the clarity of a diamond it uses **darkfield illumination**, which lights the stone from the side against a black, non-reflective background and causes the tiny inclusions and even dust particles to stand out in high relief. This can make the clarity of the diamond appear worse than it would if the light were above the stone.

When looking at jewelry with the unaided eye, you normally view it with **overhead lighting**. This lighting is above the stone (not literally over a person's head). Overhead lighting is reflected off the facets, whereas darkfield lighting is transmitted through the stone. If you ask salespeople to show you a diamond under a microscope, it's unlikely that they'll use its overhead lamp. Instead they may only have you view the stone under darkfield illumination. The inclusions will look more prominent than under overhead lights. To get a balanced perspective of the stone, also look at it with the microscope's overhead lamp and with a loupe.

Besides making flaws more prominent, darkfield illumination hides brilliance. To accurately assess the beauty and brilliance of a diamond, you should view it with overhead lighting. The quickest and easiest way to see a diamond's beauty magnified is with a good 10-power loupe.

Most of the loose diamond photographs in the first half of this book were taken with overhead lighting or a combination of transmitted light and overhead lighting because that is the way I normally looked at diamonds when I worked in the wholesale trade, I hardly ever used darkfield illumination to evaluate the quality of diamonds with a clarity grade lower than VVS clarity (very very slightly imperfect). I found darkfield illumination more helpful for detecting treatments and diamond imitations.

Besides viewing diamonds under fluorescent lighting, look at them in daylight and under incandescent light bulbs (bulbs with a metal wire that glows white-hot when an electric current is passed through it, e.g., halogen bulbs and normal household light bulbs.) The best gemstones look good under all types of light. In fact one dealer told me that the beauty of his diamonds is particularly noticeable under candlelight where they shimmer and sparkle much more than ordinary diamonds. So it's a good idea to view diamonds under a variety of lighting conditions, especially those in which they will normally be worn.

Other Tips on Viewing Diamonds

It's best to evaluate diamonds when they are unmounted because settings can hide diamond flaws and the metal reflects into the stone, affecting its apparent color. The tips below are valid whether you are viewing a loose or mounted diamond.

◆ Clean the stone with a soft cloth if it's dirty. Dirt and fingerprints hide color and brilliance.

◆ Look at the diamond first without magnification to determine your initial overall impression of it.

◆ When evaluating color, view the diamond against a non reflective white background. For example, you can fold a white business card in half and lay the diamond in the crease, or you can place the diamond in a white grading tray. View it from the side and face up. See the section on diamond color in the next chapter for more information and photos.

◆ Examine the stone under direct light and away from it. Your diamond won't always be spotlighted as you wear it. If it's of good quality, it will still look good out of direct light.

◆ Rotate the diamond and examine it from a variety of angles with and without magnification. The next four chapters will provide more information on what to look for.

◆ Pick up the stone more than once with the tweezers to view it under magnification and under a fluorescent light. The tweezers can hide a chip or a flaw on the **girdle** (outer edge around the circumference of the diamond). In addition, the diamond looks different depending on where along the girdle it is held.

◆ Compare the stone side by side with other diamonds. Nuances in color, transparency and brilliance will be more apparent. (**Transparency** refers to how clear, hazy, cloudy or opaque a gemstone is.)

◆ Every now and then, look away from the diamond at other objects to give your eyes a rest. When you focus too long on a stone, your perception of it may become distorted.

◆ Make sure you're alert and feel good when you examine diamonds. If you're tired, sick or under the influence of alcohol or drugs, your perception of color and brilliance will be impaired.

Who Should Read this Book?

This book is written for both lay people and trade professionals. When I wrote the first edition of the *Diamond Ring Buying Guide*, I intended it to be primarily for the general public. Later I learned that the trade was using it for sales training, reference and diamond courses. Several readers told me they'd like more in-depth information, so gradually my books have become more technical and trade-oriented. But they are still written in easy-to-read language that a lay person can understand. Trade terminology is explained as it is introduced; you don't have to have a prior knowledge of diamonds to understand this book.

The last half of Chapter 7 on synthetic diamonds is too technical for most consumers, but they can just skip it and go on to the next chapter.

Even though Chapter 14 ("How to Avoid Ripoffs") is specifically written for lay people, jewelers can also benefit from reading it. The three stories about consumers shopping for diamond rings can help jewelers understand what educated customers expect when they shop in their jewelry store.

Why my Diamond Books Don't Have Price Charts

Some readers have wondered why I don't include price charts in my book the *Diamond Ring Buying Guide*. It's normal to expect price lists in a buying guide or diamond handbook, but there are several good reasons why I have intentionally chosen to exclude them from my diamond books:

◆ **Price charts encourage people to ignore the quality of the cut** and buy diamonds solely on the basis of price, color, clarity, carat weight and shape. Yet cut can have a major impact on the beauty and price of your diamond.

◆ **Price charts don't take into account the place of purchase.** A diamond from a designer store or an exclusive mall will probably sell for more than one sold in a jewelry mart. When you buy a diamond, you're normally not just buying a gemstone. You're often buying service, documentation, and benefits such as guarantees or credit terms. In some cases, you may also be buying a prestigious name if the diamond is purchased in a famous name store or if it's branded.

◆ **The wholesale prices for natural diamonds are not standardized.** There are some reference price lists, but they don't necessarily indicate actual selling prices. Diamonds are not like cars with manufacturers' list prices.

At the beginning of this chapter, I mentioned that a dealer gave me a parcel price for the two diamonds I bought. If I'd offered to buy the entire parcel at a lower per carat price, I suspect this would have been possible. And if I had offered to pay for all the diamonds immediately with a check, I could have probably obtained an even lower price. So the two diamonds had a wide variety of "wholesale prices" depending on whether they were bought with lab documentation, dealer grades, no grades or by the parcel and depending on the terms of payment. Which of those prices is that dealer's wholesale price for those diamonds? If it's hard to establish one dealer's wholesale price, imagine how difficult it would be to come up with a standardized price that would be valid for all dealers throughout the world.

◆ **You can easily find actual sales prices on the Internet and in jewelry stores.** These prices are far more realistic and up-to-date than those printed in a book several months or years before you read them.

If the underlying goal of this book were to sell you a diamond, it would make sense for me to include a price list with my diamond prices, but I'm not selling diamonds. This helps me be more objective, accurate and thorough in the information I provide. My goal is to help you look at diamonds yourself and make educated decisions when you purchase them. This is a challenging task.

2

Diamond Price Factors

There are seven basic price factors for diamonds:
◆ **Color**
◆ **Carat weight**
◆ **Cut quality** (Proportions and finish)
◆ **Cutting style & stone shape**
◆ **Clarity** (Degree to which a stone is free from flaws)
◆ **Transparency** (Degree to which a stone is clear, hazy, or cloudy)
◆ **Treatment status** (Untreated or treated? What type of treatment?)

Why the 4 C's is No Longer an Adequate Pricing System

If you've shopped for diamonds, you've probably heard about the 4 C's of color, clarity, cut and carat weight. This system of explaining diamond pricing was developed by the GIA (Gemological Institute of America) in the 1950's. At that time, cloudy diamonds were considered industrial grade stones and were not set in jewelry, so transparency was not an issue. Neither was the treatment status because almost all diamonds were untreated. There were fewer faceting styles in the 1950's and no separate price lists for round, square and pear-shaped stones; therefore it didn't matter that "cut" referred to both shape and the quality of the cut.

Times have changed. Cloudy and hazy diamonds are now used in jewelry, more and more diamonds are being treated to improve their color and clarity grades, and shape is a distinct price factor from cut quality.

The 4 C's system of valuing gems is a clever, convenient way to explain gem pricing, which is why it's still the most frequently used pricing system. The problem is that it causes consumers to overlook the importance of transparency, treatment status and cut quality.

This problem is evident when customers look at mini-certs (certificates) that list the color, clarity, weight, and cut. After "cut," the cert may state, "round brilliant cut," without indicating proportion measurements. A lay person would therefore assume that the term "cut" just means shape and cutting style. But even though the quality of the cut is not indicated, it *is* a price factor; and it's separate from shape.

Likewise, transparency is separate from clarity. A diamond can be hazy or slightly cloudy and still get a high clarity grade of VS, yet it is less valuable and desirable than a highly transparent diamond. On the other hand, a diamond can have an imperfect clarity grade and be transparent. Clarity and transparency are somewhat interconnected in the lowest clarity grades of I_2 and I_3 because the large number of inclusions present in these grades can sometimes block the passage of light and prevent the diamond from appearing clear.

The seven price factors I've listed are explained in the rest of this chapter. To remember what they are, just call them the 5 C's and 2 T's.

Price Factors Explained

COLOR: Basically the less color, the higher the price (except for fancy colors). D is the highest and most rare colorless grade. As the grades descend towards Z, color increases and the price decreases. See the GIA (Gemological Institute of America) color grading scale below, which was developed in the 1950's.

D E F*	**G H I J**	**K L M**	**N to R**	**S to Z**	**Z+**
colorless	near colorless	faint yellow	very light yellow	light yellow	fancy yellow

(*Colorless for 0.50 ct or less, near colorless for heavier stones)

Each letter on the scale represents a narrow color range, not a specific point. In their diamond grading course, the GIA states that each of their masterstones "marks the highest point—or least amount of color—in that range. A diamond with slightly less color than the H masterstone is considered G-color, and so on." A GIA G-H split-grade masterstone represents the middle of the G grade. It doesn't have as much color as an H, but has more color than a straight G grade.

A diamond is not bad quality just because it's yellowish. It's simply worth less because there's a higher demand and lower supply of natural colorless diamonds.

Brown and gray diamonds are graded on the same scale, but with some modifications. GIA graders describe brown diamonds darker than K with the letter grade and an accompanying colored diamond grade: e.g. Faint brown for K to M, Very Light brown for N to R, and Light brown for S to Z. So an L-grade brown diamond would be graded as L-Faint brown. The GIA does this to distinguish brown stones darker than K in the normal range from yellow stones in that range. Light brown diamonds typically sell for less than light yellow diamonds.

The GIA grades gray diamonds with more color than the J masterstone using their fancy-color system. "So a K-color gray diamond would be graded simply as Faint gray without a letter grade." (From the GIA *Diamonds & Diamond Grading Course*, 2002.)

Diamonds with a natural body color other than light yellow, light brown or light gray are called **fancy color diamonds**. These colored diamonds may cost a lot more than those that are colorless. For example, a one-carat natural pink diamond could sell for five to fifteen times more than a D color diamond of the same size and quality.

Fancy color diamonds are graded with the diamond in the face-up position because their cut can influence the apparent color and because their price is based on the face-up color of the diamond. The more intense the color, the higher the price.

Diamonds in the color-less to light yellow range are color graded with the diamonds face down be-cause their price is based on the absence of color and because subtle nuances of color are more visible through the bottom of the diamond. (See photo of the diamonds of E to O color on the inside front cover.) You don't need a plastic grading tray for color view-ing; just fold a white bus-

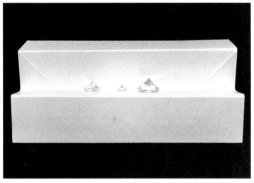

Fig. 2.1 A folded white business card makes a convenient tray for viewing diamond color. The smallest stone is a masterstone weighing 0.30 carat. The largest diamond is 4.30 carats.

iness card in half and place the diamonds in the crease on the backside.

Occasionally, diamonds in the face-up position may appear lighter or darker than their color grades. Therefore it's good to compare them face up as well as face-down. What the diamonds look like when mounted is more important than their color grade on a diamond report.

Some diamonds are colored artificially by irradiation or high-pressure high-temperature treatment. They are worth significantly less than natural color diamonds. In the GIA system, treated colored diamonds are not considered fancy diamonds. But in the trade, they're sometimes referred to as "treated (enhanced or processed) fancy diamonds."

If you are buying a diamond for yourself, it doesn't matter what color the diamond is as long as you like it. If you want a traditional type of diamond without noticeable tints of yellow, buy one with a grade higher than L color. If you like warmer colors, consider buying color grades below K color. You'll be able to get a bigger and better diamond for the same amount of money as a colorless or near colorless diamond.

If you have an ample budget and you'd like a distinctive diamond, consider getting one that's fancy color.

D–F color grades are customary for investment grade diamonds, but G–J colors are usually easier to sell because of their lower price. Fancy red, blue, pink and green diamonds can all be considered for investment. Their high prices, however, limit the number of prospective buyers.

When you evaluate diamond color, remember the following tips:

◆ Judge diamond color against a non-reflective white background. As mentioned earlier, you can fold a white business card in half and lay the diamond in the crease.

◆ Grade diamonds with a daylight equivalent fluorescent light, but before making a purchase, look at the diamonds under other lighting such as halogen spotlights, daylight by a window, and light bulbs to make sure you like their color in other environments.

◆ Use comparison diamonds to determine a precise color grade. Even professional diamond graders realize that they cannot rely only on their color memory. They need masterstones.

You can get a general idea of color without comparison stones. If you see an obvious yellowish tint when you view the stone through the side, then the stone is probably in the K to Z grade range.

◆ Make sure that the masterstones and diamonds to be graded are clean. Dirt can affect the color grade.

◆ Place your diamond both to the right and to the left of the masterstones. It's normal for it to look lighter on one side than the other because of an optical illusion called the "master-eye effect."

◆ Be careful not to mistakenly downgrade larger diamonds. They often appear darker than small masterstones of the same color grade because the color appears to deepen when it is viewed through a larger medium.

◆ Keep in mind that precise color grading can only be done with loose diamonds. The color of the metal surrounding diamonds set in jewelry influences the appearance of the diamonds. Consequently, their color can only be estimated.

For more information on diamond color, consult the *Diamond Ring Buying Guide* by Renée Newman and *Collecting and Classifying Coloured Diamonds* by Stephen C. Hofer.

CARAT WEIGHT: In most cases, the higher the carat weight category, the greater the per-carat price of the diamond. A carat is a unit of weight equaling 1/5 of a gram. The weight of small diamonds is frequently expressed in points, with one point equaling 0.01 ct (carat). In diamond districts, you may hear the term **grainer**. This is a word that is used to describe the weights of diamond in multiples of 0.25 ct (one grain). A four grainer is a 1 ct diamond.

If a diamond is advertised as weighing ".25 points," this can be misread as being .25 ct in weight when in fact .25 points is equal to 1/400 of a carat instead of " 1/4 carat." Pay close attention to the way diamond weight is described before making a purchase.

Consumers may also misread the labels **1 ct TW** (one carat total weight) and **1 ct** (the weight of one stone). A ring with a **1 ct** top quality diamond can be worth more than 10 times as much as a ring with 1 ct TW of diamonds of the same quality.

When you shop for diamonds, think in terms of the per-carat cost. This is what diamond dealers do. To calculate the total cost of a diamond, use the equation: **Total cost of a stone = carat weight x per-carat cost**

Diamonds can be divided into weight categories. These categories often vary from one dealer to another but may be outlined as follows:

Table 2.1 Weight Categories for Diamonds		
0.01 – 0.03 ct	0.30 – 0.37 ct	0.96 – 0.99 ct
0.04 – 0.07 ct	0.38 – 0.45 ct	1.00 – 1.49 ct
0.08 – 0.14 ct	0.46 – 0.49 ct	1.50 – 1.99 ct
0.15 – 0.17 ct	0.50 – 0.69 ct	2.00 – 2.49 ct
0.18 – 0.22 ct	0.70 – 0.89 ct	2.50 – 2.99 ct
0.23 – 0.29 ct	0.90 – 0.95 ct	3.00 – 3.99 ct

The above weight categories are based mainly on those listed in the *Rapaport Diamond Report*. As diamonds move up from one weight category to another, their prices may increase from about 5% to 50%. So if you buy, for example, a 0.97 ct diamond instead of a 1 ct, you'll normally pay less per carat, even though the stone will resemble a one-carat diamond. Low-quality diamonds tend to show less of a price differential between categories than those of high quality, especially at the jump from just less than 1 ct to 1 ct or more.

Usually the greater the weight, the greater the rarity, which is one reason for price jumps when diamonds move from one weight category to another. But demand also plays a role. One caraters and half caraters are in high demand so there can be a considerable price jump when diamonds move to these categories. In the 1980's when tennis bracelets were unusually popular, three pointers (0.03-carat diamonds) actually cost more per carat than five pointers because the three pointers were more in demand.

It doesn't matter what size diamond you buy if you're going to wear it in jewelry. One carat or larger is the norm for investment diamonds, with the exception of rare fancy color diamonds, which may weigh less. Virtually any size can be resold if necessary.

CUT QUALITY: (Proportions and finish, also called **make**): This is a crucial factor, which can affect prices by as much as 50%. Two of the main considerations of cut are:

1. **Do you see brilliance all across the stone when you look at the diamond face up** (figs. 2.2 & 2.3)? Diamond brilliance should not be interrupted by dark areas (fig.2.4).
2. **Are you paying for excess weight?** (fig. 2.5)

Fig. 2.2 Emerald cut with good brilliance

Fig. 2.3 Radiant cut with good brilliance

Fig. 2.4 Diamond with a dark center

Fig. 2.5 Diamond with excess weight

Judge cut with the unaided eye and a 10x magnifier. Chapters 3 and 4 explain cut evaluation in detail.

CUTTING STYLE & STONE SHAPE: Currently rounds cost more than pear and marquise shapes and emerald cuts. The effect of shape on price varies depending on the stone size, demand and available supply. For example, there have been periods in the past where marquise shapes have sold for more than rounds.

While I was writing this book, an appraiser in Canada told me that princess cuts (square shapes) were in high demand in her area and were selling for more than rounds. Normally square shapes can cost as much as 15–30% less than rounds because there is less weight loss from the rough when cutting squares and there is usually less of a demand for squares. Four common diamond shapes are shown below:

Fig 2.6 Marquise (brilliant cut)

Fig. 2.7 Princess cut (square brilliant)

Fig. 2.8 Pear shape (brilliant cut)

Fig. 2.9 Oval (brilliant cut)

The preceding shapes can be cut with various faceting styles. The GIA has simplified the description of these cutting styles by limiting them to three basic types—step cut, brilliant cut and mixed cut.

Step Cut: Has rows of facets that are usually four-sided and elongated and parallel to the girdle (figs. 2.10). If step-cuts have clipped-off corners, they're called **emerald cuts** because emeralds are often cut this way (fig. 2.2. This protects the corners and provides places where prongs can secure the stone. Emerald cuts are in essence step-cut, octagonal rectangles. They tend to have more facets than baguettes. Emerald-cut diamonds are usually rectangular or square, but they can also be triangular (fig. 2.11).

Fig. 2.10 Step-cut rectangle

Fig 2.11 Step-cut triangle

Fig. 2.12 Trilliant (brilliant cut)

Brilliant Cut: Has triangular-, kite-, or lozenge-shaped facets that radiate outward around the stone. Figures 2.6 to 2.9 & 2.12 are examples of brilliant cuts. The jewelry trade generally refers to round diamonds with 58 facets as **full cuts** or traditional **round brilliants**.

Fig. 2.13 Round brilliant

Fig. 2.14 Mixed cut Lucere® diamond from Ernest Slotar, Inc.

Mixed Cut: Has both step- and brilliant-cut facets. The pavilion, for example, can be step cut and the crown can be brilliant cut, but the step-

and brilliant-cut facets can also be scattered over the diamond. This cut is used a lot more on transparent colored stones than on diamonds, but some of the new branded diamonds are mixed cuts.

Brilliant-cut square diamonds (princess cuts) may cost slightly more than step-cut squares, depending on size. They have the same shape but different faceting styles. Patented and trademarked cutting styles typically sell for more than generic cuts of the same shape.

The most dramatic impact of stone shape and cutting style on price is with fancy color diamonds because their face-up color can be intensified by the shape and faceting style, and because the rough is so expensive. For example, a 1-carat, intense-yellow round diamond can cost from 10% to over 100% more than a radiant with the same weight and color grade, depending on the stones and the dealer selling them. This is because the rough of the round diamond must be darker than that of the radiant to achieve the same intense yellow face-up color; cutters can't play as much with the angles and shape of rounds to maximize their color. The stronger the color of the rough, the higher the price of the rough. The final price of the diamond is based largely on the cost of the rough.

CLARITY: (The degree to which a stone is free from external marks called **blemishes** and internal features called **inclusions**).There are eleven GIA clarity grades, which are defined in the chart below:

GIA CLARITY GRADES*	
* For trained graders using 10-power magnification and proper lighting	
Fl	**Flawless**, no blemishes or inclusions.
IF	**Internally flawless**, no inclusions and only insignificant blemishes.
VVS$_1$ & VVS$_2$	**Very, very slightly included**, minute inclusions that are difficult to see.
VS$_1$ & VS$_2$	**Very slightly included**, minor inclusions ranging from difficult to somewhat easy to see.
SI$_1$ & SI$_2$	**Slightly included**, noticeable inclusions that are easy (SI$_1$) or very easy (SI$_2$) to see.
I$_1$, I$_2$, & I$_3$ In Europe: P$_1$, P$_2$ & P$_3$	**Imperfect**, obvious inclusions that usually are eye-visible face up; in I$_3$, distinctions are based on the combined effect on durability, transparency, and brilliance.

Photo examples of eight clarity grades are shown in Chapter 5 of this book and in Chapter 7 of the *Diamond Ring Buying Guide.*

Lay people often refer to inclusions as "flaws" and "imperfections." Gemologists usually prefer not to use these terms because of their negative connotations. This book sometimes uses the term "flaw" because it's easy for a lay person to understand, and it's a short word that includes both inclusions and blemishes. The fewer, smaller and less noticeable the flaws, the better the clarity and the higher the price of the stone.

When you examine diamonds under magnification, you will see a variety of inclusions and blemishes. They are described below.

Diamond Inclusions

◆ **Crystals** of all sorts of interesting shapes and sizes are commonly seen in diamonds (figs. 2.15 & 2.16). Over 24 different minerals have been identified as crystal inclusions in diamonds, but the most frequent type crystal seen is another diamond. Minute crystals that look like small specks under 10-power magnification are called **pinpoints**. Crystals can lower the clarity grade of your diamond, but they can also turn it into a collector's item if they are unusual and attractive. The larger and more obvious crystals are, the more they impact the clarity grade.

◆ **Cracks** of various sizes are also common in diamonds. They may also be called **fissures** or **breaks**. When they follow the grain of the diamond, they're called **cleavages,** and appear straight and flat. Cracks that are not cleavages are called **fractures**.

On lab reports, cracks are usually identified as feathers. In their diamond grading course, the GIA states that "a **feather** is a general term for any break in a diamond" (pg 18, lesson 10, 2002 course). Diamonds with insignificant feathers can receive VS clarity grades.

The girdle (outer edge) of diamonds often has tiny hairline cleavages, which are called **bearding** (fig 2.26). Light bearding does not prevent a diamond from receiving a clarity grade of VVS (very very slightly included). Tiny cracks are normal diamond features.

Larger cracks like the one in figure 2.19 have a more serious effect on the clarity grade because they are more noticeable and they can sometimes threaten the stone's durability.

◆ **Clouds** are hazy or milky areas in a diamond (fig. 2.20). Most clouds are made up of crystals too tiny to see individually under 10-power magnification. Clouds may be hard to find in diamonds with high clarity grades. When clouds are large and dense, they diminish transparency and make your diamond look undesirably white.

Fig 2.15 Crystal inclusion

Fig. 2.16 Black and clear crystals and feathers

Fig. 2.17 A minor cleavage (feather)

Fig. 2.18 Same cleavage from another angle

Fig. 2.19 A serious crack (feather)

Fig. 2.20 Pinpoints and a cloud

◆ **Growth or grain lines** are fine lines or ripples caused by irregular crystallization (fig. 2.21). They are also referred to as twinning lines. Sometimes diamonds look hazy or oily when many of these lines are present. White, colored or reflective graining can affect the clarity grade. Colorless graining does not normally lower the clarity grade but it can sometimes affect the transparency and brilliance of a diamond.

◆ **Cavities** are spaces left when a surface-reaching crystal comes out during polishing or when part of a feather breaks away and leaves a deep, angular opening. **Chips** often occur along the girdle (fig. 2,22)

◆ **Knots** are included diamond crystals that are left exposed on the surface by polishing. They may look like raised areas on the diamond, and there may be a difference in polish quality between the knot and the surrounding areas when examined with reflected light.

◆ **Laser drill holes** are tiny holes drilled into the diamond with a laser beam, allowing black spots to be dissolved or bleached out with chemicals (fig 2.23). This treatment normally improves the appearance. There are times, however, when the diamond looks worse after drilling due to the resulting long white drill holes. To see laser holes you usually have to tilt the diamond or view it from the side.

Surface Blemishes

◆ **Scratches, nicks, pits and abraded facet edges** are not considered as serious as inclusions because they can often be polished away.

◆ **Extra facets** are additions to the normal number of facets (flat, geometric diamond surfaces) (fig 2.25). They are usually added to polish away a flaw. This helps retain weight by avoiding the alternative of repolishing the regular facet.. They don't affect the clarity grade of a diamond if they are on the pavilion and can't be seen face up at 10-power magnification.

◆ **Naturals** are part of the original surface of the diamond crystal left unpolished (fig. 2.26). Sometimes they have step-like ridges or triangular forms (called **trigons**) on them that help indicate your stone is truly a diamond. Naturals don't affect the clarity grade if they're confined to the girdle and don't distort the girdle outline.

Some people wonder if laser inscriptions on the girdle (rim around the stone) are inclusions. They're not, and they do not affect the clarity grade or damage the diamond. The inscriptions, which may consist of numbers, logo, pictures, and/or words, are confined to the girdle and are so small that you normally have to view them at 25-power magnification in order to read them. A 10-power loupe is not strong enough. The inscriptions are engraved on the diamond with a laser.

Fig 2.21   Grain lines

Fig. 2.22   Large chip

Fig. 2.23   Laser drill holes

Fig. 2.24   Abraded facet edges and pits

Fig. 2.25   Extra facets

Fig. 2.26   Natural and bearding

Fig. 2.27 Laser inscription. *Diamond from J Landau, photo by Derse Studio.*

Fig. 2.28 Same inscription at lower magnification. *From Landau, photo: Derse Studio.*

Figure 2.27 shows the highly magnified (at least 25-power) numbers that correspond to an AGSL (American Gem Society Laboratory) diamond report. To give you a better idea of how small the numbers are, they are shown in figure 2.28 at a lower magnification. Laser inscriptions are also used for personal message such as "I love you."

Consumers are sometimes afraid of leaving their diamonds for repair for fear of having the diamonds switched. Thanks to laser inscriptions they can have peace of mind. The jeweler can show them the diamond under a microscope after the diamond comes back for repair and have the customer match the number on their lab report to the numbers on the diamond girdle. Another method is to compare the map of the inclusions on the diamond report to the inclusions in the diamond. It's possible to match the inclusions with a loupe, but it is easier with a microscope. Depending on how the diamond is mounted, it might also be possible to measure the diamond and compare its measurements to those on the diamond report.

TRANSPARENCY: The GIA and the classic book *Gems* by Robert Webster define transparency as the degree to which a gemstone transmits light. They list five categories of transparency.

◆ **Transparent**—objects seen through the gemstone look clear and distinct.

◆ **Semi-transparent**—objects look slightly hazy or blurry through the stone.

◆ **Translucent**—objects are vague and hard to see. Imagining what it is like to read print through frosted glass will help you understand the concept of translucency.

◆ **Semi-translucent or semi-opaque**—only a small fraction of light passes through the stone, mainly around the edges.

◆ **Opaque**—virtually no light can pass through the gemstone.

Fig 2.29 Diamond with high transparency

Fig. 2.30 Sub-microscopic particles make this diamond look cloudy.

Fig. 2.31 Visible inclusions seriously affect the transparency of this I₃ diamond.

Fig. 2.32 Internal graining gives this diamond an oily appearance.

Fig. 2.33 This diamond only has a few pinpoint inclusions under 10x. However it is slightly cloudy, so it's not as valuable as a highly transparent diamond of the same clarity grade.

Fig. 2.34 A cloudy diamond with a cloud in the center

Mineralogists use the term **diaphaneity**, but gemologists prefer the term "transparency" because it's easier for lay people to understand. Another word that refers to transparency is **texture.** AGL (American Gemological Laboratories) in New York applies this term to fine particles that interrupt the passage of light in a material. Jade dealers often use the term **translucency** and other colored gem dealers use the term **crystal.**

I first became aware of the importance of transparency when a New York colored-gem dealer, Jack Abraham, mentioned that I had left the concept out of my book *The Ruby & Sapphire Buying Guide.* Consequently, I added a section on transparency to all of my colored gem books and I eventually included the concept in the Sixth Edition of the *Diamond Ring Buying Guide.*

Transparency can play a major role in determining the value and desirability of a gemstone. In most cases, the higher the transparency the more valuable the gemstone.

Diamonds from the Golconda mine in India are noted for having an extraordinary transparency. As a result, the term "Golconda" is occasionally used to describe a highly transparent diamond.

Clarity and transparency are interconnected, but they're different. If there's a cloudy spot in a transparent diamond, the cloud is a clarity feature. If the entire diamond is cloudy due to submicroscopic inclusions, then the cloudiness is a matter of transparency. However, this should also affect the clarity grade of the diamond.

In most cases, clarity grades will not help you select transparent diamonds because:

◆ Clarity grades don't normally take into account subtle differences in transparency.

◆ Diamonds with obvious transparency problems are seldom submitted to labs for grading. More often than not they're mounted in bargain-priced jewelry.

If you'd like to buy a brilliant diamond, select one with good transparency. This is not hard for a layperson to do. Just look at the diamond at different angles and check to see if it's as clear as crystal glass or pure water. Face-up the diamond should be brilliant and there should be a strong contrast between the dark and bright areas.

When judging transparency, make sure the diamond is clean; examine it both with your naked eye and a 10-power magnifier, and look at it under different lighting conditions (fluorescent light, incandescent light, sunlight, and away from light). Keep in mind that white objects or walls can reflect into the diamond making it appear less transparent than it really is. It is helpful to have a transparent diamond sample for comparison. Nuances of transparency and haziness are more easily detected, and your evaluation will be more accurate.

You won't need a comparison stone or magnification to spot diamonds with serious transparency problems. You can see their cloudiness from several feet away. If the diamonds don't sparkle or shine even under the store's special spotlights, there is definitely a problem. The diamonds will probably look worse away from the lights.

Diamonds with dirt and fingerprints may resemble low-grade milky diamonds. Therefore, after you receive or purchase diamond jewelry, clean it regularly; you'll be able to appreciate more the brilliance and beauty of your diamonds.

TREATMENT STATUS: Unlike colored gems, most diamonds are untreated. However, that is changing. Diamonds may undergo the following treatments to improve their clarity, color, transparency, and marketability:

Fracture filling: A method of improving clarity and transparency by filling cracks with a substance that makes them almost invisible. The cleavages that are filled in diamonds are not large gaps; they are extremely narrow. The filler used is a thin glass-like film, so the filling process does not add measurable weight to the stone. Even though you may not see them, the filled cracks are still present in the diamond. Two other names for the diamond filling process are **glass infilling** and **clarity enhancement**.

Laser drilling: A treatment that gets rid of dark inclusions. A laser beam is used to drill a narrow hole to the dark area in the diamond. If the inclusion is not vaporized by the laser itself, then it's dissolved or bleached with acid. After the treatment, the hole looks like a white dot face-up and like a thin white line from the side-view of the stone. If the hole is filled, it can be as hard to spot as a filled fracture. Such a stone is considered to be both drilled and filled. Laser drilling is also called a clarity enhancement.

Coating: The application of a colored substance (usually bluish) to the surface of a diamond to improve the color grade. A fluoride coating such as that applied to lenses can mask a diamond's yellow body color. Usually the coating is applied to the pavilion (bottom), but occasionally it's applied thinly only at or near the girdle. Diamonds have also been coated with colored nail polish, enamel and other substances. Sometimes a tiny amount of blue ink is applied to the girdle under the prongs to improve the apparent color.

Since coatings on diamonds are not permanent, they're not an accepted form of treatment. Coating is usually considered a deceptive trade practice, and is therefore not disclosed. It's detected with magnification, solvents and color filters. However, detection can be difficult. You can avoid buying coated diamonds by dealing with reputable jewelers and by getting a lab report or appraisal from qualified professionals.

Irradiation + Heating: A dual process used to change light yellow and brown diamonds into green, blue, yellow, orange, black (very dark green) and occasionally pink, purple, or red-colored diamonds. Irradiation is usually followed by heating at about 800°–1000°C to improve the irradiated colors, which are often very dark. The color of irradiated diamonds is basically stable, but some stones can change color if they come into contact with a jeweler's torch.

High Pressure High Temperature (HPHT) Treatment: A process used to change the color of diamonds by heating diamonds to temperatures above 1900°C under extreme pressure. It can turn inexpensive brown diamonds colorless or make them green, yellow, blue, red or pink. The color is stable.

The main advantage to buying treated diamonds is price. Dealer Paul Reiser, who specializes in selling second-hand diamonds, says that laser-drilled stones are typically discounted 25 to 30 % and fracture-filled ones often sell at 40% off of the secondary market price of untreated stones.

Diamonds colored by irradiation or HPHT treatment are a fraction of the cost of natural fancy color diamonds. For example, a one-carat irradiated "fancy" green diamond of VS clarity may retail for $3000 to $4000 per carat. If the same diamond were of natural color, it would probably sell for over $100,000 per carat because natural green diamonds are unusually rare. In October 1999, a 0.90-carat vivid green diamond was auctioned for $736,111. Treated green diamonds are much easier to find and are often produced from low-priced diamonds that are brownish or below L color. In essence, the customer is paying for the cost of the low-priced diamond and the treatment process.

One reason people purchase my books is for advice in buying. If you plan on reselling a diamond or on trading it in later for a larger or higher quality diamond, buy untreated diamonds. They are always in demand and you can resell them in any type of market. Treated diamonds are hard to resell.

If you're buying a bridal diamond for an everyday ring, an untreated diamond is likely to be more durable and resistant to abrasions than fracture-filled diamonds or HPHT treated diamonds. High temperature heat treatment has made some colored gemstones more brittle and susceptible to chipping and abrasions. We don't know yet what effect it has on the durability of diamonds. Likewise, you can't be certain if fracture-filled diamonds are resistant to knocks, a normal occurrence when they're mounted in everyday rings. Diamonds with large fractures and cleavages, be they filled or unfilled, are not as durable as diamonds of good clarity. One of the main advantages of buying diamonds for bridal rings, instead of other gems is that untreated diamonds are more resistant to abrasions and damage. They have withstood the test of time.

Treated diamonds can be an affordable option to buying untreated ones. They can allow you to get a big look or unusual colors at a low price. However, if there's not a significant price difference between the enhanced or unenhanced stones, you are better off buying untreated diamonds.

Fracture filling, laser drilling and coatings can be detected by jewelers and appraisers. Accurate detection of irradiation and high temperature heat treatment normally requires the special expertise and sophisticated equipment of a qualified independent gem laboratory. An important reason for buying a diamond accompanied by a lab report is to verify that the diamond is untreated. Labs are able to identify the vast majority of treated diamonds, but some irradiated and HPHT diamonds are not detectable. Therefore if a lab does not have evidence proving a diamond is untreated, they include a statement such as "color origin undeterminable." There are probably cases, however, where diamond color is misidentified as natural when in fact it's the result of treatment.

If you're buying an untreated diamond, have it identified as untreated on the receipt. If a stone is identified as enhanced or processed, this means it is treated. Attractive untreated diamonds are still readily available. They will continue to be available if consumers ask for them.

Other Sources of Photos and Information on Diamonds

This chapter is a summary of what you should look for when buying diamonds. To get a better understanding, read the rest of this book and examine the photos. Then cover up the captions and see if you can interpret the photos by yourself. Additional photo examples will be helpful. You'll find them in the following publications, which are all excellent references.

Collecting & Classifying Coloured Diamonds by Stephen Hofer: Ashland Press.
Diamond Grading ABC by Verena Pagel-Theisen: Rubin & Son
Diamond Ring Buying Guide by Renée Newman: Intl. Jewelry Publications
The MicroWorld of Diamonds by John Koivula: Gemworld International
Photo Masters For Diamond Grading by Gary Roskin: Gemworld International

Photos and information on the latest research about diamonds:
Australian Gemmologist. Gemmological Association of Australia, Brisbane
Gems & Gemology. Gemological Institute of America, Carlsbad, CA
Journal of Gemmology. Gemmological Association and Gem Testing Laboratory
    of Great Britain, London

3

Judging the Cut of Fancy Shapes

In the previous chapter, I stated that there are two fundamental considerations when assessing the cut quality of a diamond:

1. Do you see brilliance all across the diamond when it is face up?
2. Are you paying for excess weight?

Some trade members would include proportion measurements, shape outline and symmetry in the above list. However, I think this confuses consumers, especially when evaluating **fancy shapes** (any shape other than round). In my opinion, it's more important to be able to spot good light refraction in gemstones than to determine their length to width ratios and proportion measurements. Nevertheless, in the next chapter I will address some of these other issues in order to help you understand diamond grading reports and some of the finer details of diamond grading.

Before I discuss how to evaluate cut, let me explain some basic terminology:

Facets	The flat, polished surfaces or planes on a diamond
Table	The large, flat, top facet. It has an octagonal shape on a round brilliant diamond.
Culet	The tiny facet on the pointed bottom of the pavilion, parallel to the table
Girdle	The narrow rim around the diamond. The girdle plane is parallel to the table and is the largest diameter of any part of the stone.
Crown	The upper part of the diamond above the girdle
Crown height	The distance between the girdle and table planes
Pavilion	The lower part of the diamond below the girdle. It's cone-shaped on a round diamond.
Pavilion depth	The distance from the girdle plane to the culet
Brilliant cut	The most common style of diamond cutting. The standard brilliant cut consists of 32 facets plus a table above the girdle and 24 facets plus a culet below the girdle. Other shapes besides round can be faceted as brilliant cuts.

Figure 3.1 illustrates some of the preceding terms and serves as an example of a well-proportioned round brilliant.

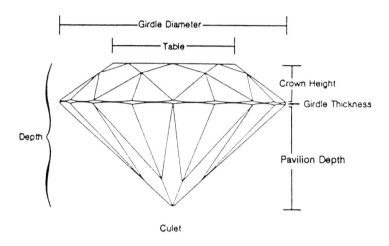

Fig. 3.1 Profile of a well-cut round brilliant diamond

Judging Cut Quality

I believe the first thing you should look for in a diamond is brilliance. Ideally the brilliance will be even throughout the stone. It's easiest to achieve this with a round diamond.

The diamond in figure 3.2 is an example of a gemstone with even brilliance. Notice the black triangular patterns interspersed throughout the diamond. Patterns similar to this are normal in well-cut diamonds providing the black areas are tiny, as in this diamond. In fact, their presence helps create a sparkle effect (technically called **scintillation)** because as the diamond or light moves, the dark areas shift

Fig 3.2 Diamond with high brilliance. *Royal Brilliant®* *photo from Exroyal Co, Inc.*

from black to white making the brilliance appear to twinkle. The shape and size of the facets plays a major role in determining the degree of scintillation.

Even though this diamond is not an "ideal cut," its cut quality and brilliance are excellent. ("Ideal cut" is a marketing term used for well-cut diamonds that conform to a set of proportions that are described in the next chapter.) Diamonds do not have to be "ideal cuts" to be ideally cut.

It's more difficult to produce fancy shape diamonds with even brilliance than rounds. Each shape requires a different set of cutting angles to achieve maximum brilliance. Even though some dealers and appraisers have published recommended angles and proportions, there is no universal set of standards for cutting fancy shapes.

When evaluating the cut and brilliance of a fancy shape diamond, look for the following features, which are described afterwards in more detail:

♦ **Large dark black areas**, which are often in the shape of a bow tie, cross, or circle

♦ **"Windows"**—a clear or washed out area in the middle of the diamond that allows you to see right through the stone

♦ **Fisheye**—A white donut shaped girdle reflection

All three of these characteristics indicate diminished brilliance.

Bow Ties and Other Dark Patterns

If the pavilions (bottoms) of fancy shape diamonds are too deep or improperly proportioned, the stones may display a gray to black bow tie form across the width of the stone when viewed face up. Some squarish shapes may show a cross pattern and rounds can have a dark circular center. The larger and darker the bow tie, the less desirable the stone. Most fancy-shaped diamonds have at least a slight bow tie, but when it is so pronounced that it is distracting, the bow tie lowers the value of the stone.

Figures 3.3 to 3.14 show several examples of well-cut diamonds next to those with dark patterns. After you examine them, visit a few jewelry stores and look at some fancy shaped diamonds. Check if there is brilliance all across the stone or if it is interrupted with dark areas. Finding well-cut

Fig. 3.3 Emerald cut with a large bow tie

Fig. 3.4 Emerald cut with good brilliance

fancy shapes can be a challenge, but such stones are available. The manufacturer of the Cushette® in figure 3.6 told me that one of the distinguishing features of their branded cuts is that they do not have bow ties.

Fig. 3.5 A cushion-shape diamond with a moderate bow tie.

Fig. 3.6 Diamond with good brilliance and no bow tie. *Cushette® photo from Diamco.*

Fig. 3.7 Brilliant-cut square (princess-cut) with some dark areas

Fig. 3.8 A better brilliant-cut square. *Quadrillion® photo from Bez Ambar.*

Fig. 3.9 Tapered baguette with low brilliance

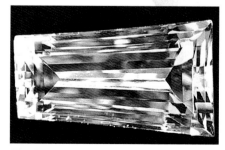

Fig. 3.10 Diamond with higher brilliance.

Fig. 3.11 Pear shape with a bow tie

Fig. 3.12 Pear shape with a minimal bow tie

Fig. 3.13 A distracting black cross. Compare it to the more brilliant diamond in figure 3.14.

Fig. 3.14 Flanders Ideal Square Cut®. *Photo from National Diamond Syndicate.*

TEST: Which diamond below is better cut and displays more brilliance? (See next page for answer.)

Fig. 3.15 Christmas tree diamond

Fig. 3.16 Diamond star

If you answered that the diamond star is better cut and more brilliant than the Christmas tree, then you have proved that you're capable of making visual judgments about diamond cut. You didn't need proportion measurements, a cut grade, or a lab document to determine that the large dark areas in the tree diamond reduced its brilliance. You were able to determine this with your eyes. In this case, magnification isn't necessary, but sometimes a loupe can help magnify the beauty of a diamond and help you detect finer nuances of brilliance. Comparison stones can also help.

Windows

When gemstones are improperly cut and are viewed face up, they may display a **window**— a clear or washed out area in the middle of the stone that allows you to see right through it. Windows (or windowing) can occur in any transparent, faceted stone no matter how light or dark it is and no matter how deep or shallow its pavilion. In general, the larger the window, the poorer the cut. Windowed stones are the attempt of the cutter to maximize weight at the expense of brilliance.

Windows are seldom seen in diamonds because of their high refractive index (the degree to which light is bent as it passes through the stone), but they are frequently seen in colored gemstones. When windows occur in diamonds, they are usually seen in emerald cuts and other step cuts (figure 3.17). Since diamonds are often mounted with colored gems, it's important to know how to evaluate them too, especially considering that few labs supply cut quality information on their colored gem reports. If you learn how to spot windows, this will help you select gems with good brilliance.

Fig. 3.17 A small window in an emerald cut diamond through which print is visible.

Fig. 3.18 Similar shaped diamond with no window. *Lucére® Diamond; photo from Ernest Slotar, Inc.*

To look for windows, hold the stone about an inch or two (2 to 5 cm) above a contrasting background such as your hand or a piece of white paper. Then try to look straight through the top of the stone without tilting it, and check if you can see the background or a light window-like area in the center of it.

If the stone is light colored, you might try holding it above a printed page to see if the print shows through. If the center area of the stone is pale or lifeless compared to a darker faceted area surrounding the pale center, this is also a window effect. To better understand windowing, compare the two stones below to the ones in figure 3.21.

Fig. 3.19 Moderate window in a sapphire

Fig. 3.20 Large window in an amethyst

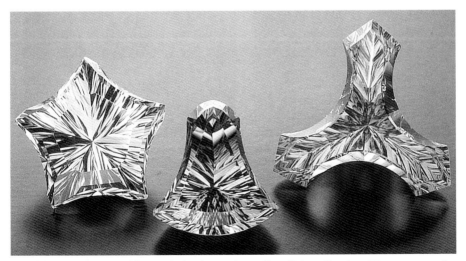

Fig. 3.21 Gemstones with no windowing and excellent light refraction. They were cut by Mark Gronlund. Even though their proportions may not meet traditional standards, they are well cut.

Fisheyes

Sometimes the face-up view of a diamond displays a white circle resembling a skinny donut (figs. 3.22 & 3.23). In the trade, this is called a **fisheye**. It's caused by the reflection of the girdle (outer diamond edge) when the pavilion is too shallow. A large table (top center facet) can make a fisheye more noticeable. The thicker and more prominent the white circle, the poorer the cut. Besides looking bad, fisheye diamonds usually lack the brilliance of those that are well-cut.

When I worked in the trade and sorted diamonds, I was told to treat strong fisheyes like the one in figure 3.23 as rejection quality diamonds because of their diminished brilliance. Although I only have photo examples of round fisheye diamonds, I've seen many fisheye effects in diamonds of a wide variety of shapes. Round brilliant fisheyes are more likely to be seen in stones under 0.20 carats, but they are found in larger sizes as well. Fisheyes can have a strong negative impact on diamond value.

To detect fisheyes, look at the diamond face up with a loupe and tilt it slightly. Fine-cut diamonds do not display a fisheye effect, not even when slightly tilted.

Fig. 3.22 Narrow fisheve in a single cut (a cutting style with 16 facets and a table)

Fig. 3.23 Strong fisheye in a round brilliant cut diamond

Excess Diamond Weight

If you are looking at two one-carat diamonds of similar quality and one of them has an extremely thick girdle (the rim around the edge of the diamond) and the other has a proper size medium girdle, the diamond with the extremely thick girdle will look noticeably smaller. The price of the

Fig. 3.24 Profile of a fancy-shape diamond with excess weight around the girdle area. Face up this diamond looks small for its weight.

Fig. 3.25 Profile of a well-cut round brilliant cut diamond

diamond with the extremely thick girdle will probably be lower, but this does not mean it is a better buy. It costs less because it has a lot of unnecessary weight around the girdle area, which does not increase its brilliance and sparkle. In fact, the thicker girdle may even detract from its brilliance. The face-up size of a diamond is more important than its weight. Therefore in addition to checking for face-up brilliance, you should look at diamonds from the side to verify that they do not have a lot of unnecessary weight.

Fig. 3.26 A very thick faceted girdle

Sometimes people mistakenly think a big spread (a larger face-up size is always desirable. Diamonds with windows and fish-eye effects typically have shallow pavilions, which makes them appear bigger than well-cut diamonds. However, if your goal is to purchase a beautiful diamond, you

Fig. 3.28 Lengthwise view of a marquise with a profile that is too flat for adequate brilliance and a crown that is too thin to provide proper sparkle and fire. Face up the diamond looks big for its weight.

Fig. 3.27 Top heavy old mine cut

should buy one that was cut to maximize brilliance. Thin crowns and large tables will also help increase the face-up size, but at the expense of sparkle and **fire** (rainbow colors that form when light strikes a prism, technically called **dispersion**. See figure 3.28 for an example of a thin crown.

Figure 3.27 is an example of a diamond with a crown that is too high. Even though this is an old mine cut, which is explained in Chapter 9, modern-cut diamonds are sometimes cut with very high crowns in order to maximize weight retention of the rough.

Bulging pavilions are another sign of cutters placing more emphasis on weight retention than on beauty. When diamonds have thick girdles, high crowns or bulging pavilions, dealers call them heavy makes. Even though excess weight can often be detected from the face up view, it's easiest for lay people to see it in the profile view. It can play a major role in the price of a diamond.

The next chapter will explain pavilion measurements for round brilliants. Do not use those measurements to assess fancy shapes. They must be cut to different depths than rounds to prevent fisheyes and dark areas. For example, brilliant-cut triangles are normally cut more shallow than rounds, whereas squares are typically cut deeper.

Adam Daniels at Ernest Slotar, Inc. says that their Lucére Diamond (figure 3.18) must have a total depth averaging about 70% in order to maximize brilliance, unlike round brilliants which should have a total depth percentage closer to 60%. Because fancy shapes differ in their proportion requirements and because trade preferences vary, I have not discussed proportions in this chapter. It's more important that you look at the diamond face up and from the side and evaluate it visually.

I did not discuss shape outline and length to width ratios in this chapter because I believe that is largely a matter of personal choice. However, diamonds which conform to traditional shape outlines, such as the ones below, are often in higher demand and may therefore cost more.

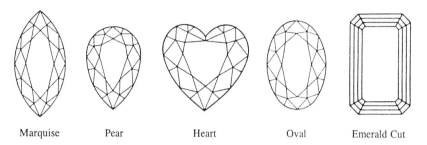

Marquise   Pear   Heart   Oval   Emerald Cut

Fig. 3.29 *Diagrams courtesy of the Gemological Institute of America*

My book the *Diamond Ring Buying Guide* briefly covers the topic of shape outlines in the chapter on "Shape & Cutting Style." You'll find a lot more information about it on the Internet. What's difficult to find is advice on judging brilliance, which, in my opinion, is the most important part of diamond evaluation.

4

Judging Cut (Round Brilliants)

In the previous chapter, I discussed two fundamental concepts of diamond cut evaluation.
1. Face-up brilliance
2. Excess weight (e.g., thick girdles, bulging pavilions)

In this chapter, I'll provide more details on judging the proportions of the:
◆ Pavilion
◆ Crown
◆ Table
◆ Girdle
◆ Culet

In addition, I'll discuss **finish,** which consists of two subcategories:
◆ Symmetry
◆ Polish

Pavilion

The pavilion (bottom of the diamond) plays the most important role in determining brilliance—the amount of light reflected back to the eye. If the pavilion is too shallow, a fisheye effect (white donut-shaped circle) will be visible (fig. 4.2) and there will be decreased brilliance. Some diamond dealers describe these diamonds as being "flat." The term "flat" is also associated with very thin crowns.

If the pavilion is too deep, the diamond will look dark in the center (fig. 4.3). Diamonds with black centers are called **nailheads**.

You don't need to know the proportions of a diamond to determine if it has an acceptable pavilion depth. Just look at the diamond face up both with and without a loupe, and verify that it has good even brilliance. If it does not look dark in the center and has no fisheye effect even when you tilt it slightly, the pavilion depth is acceptable.

If you are only interested in visually evaluating diamonds, then skip to the next section, which discusses the crown. The information in the rest of this section is for people who want to understand pavilion data on lab reports.

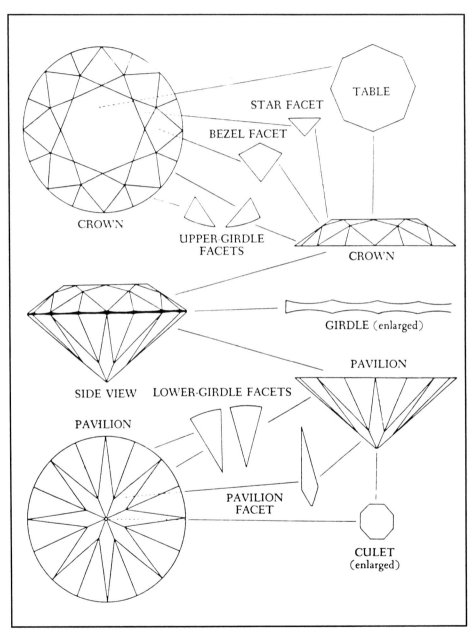

Fig. 4.1 Facet arrangement of a standard round brilliant cut. *Diagram reprinted with permission from the Gemological Institute of America.*

Fig. 4.2 A fisheye in a round brilliant with a pavilion that is too shallow.

Fig. 4.3 Round brilliant with a dark center a deep pavilion and very large table

On their diamond grading reports, a few labs indicate the **pavilion depth percentage**—the distance from the girdle plane to the culet, expressed as a percentage of the average girdle diameter. When the pavilion depth percentage falls below 41%, a fisheye will start to form. The lower the percentage, the stronger the fisheye will be. In other words, the shallower the pavilion, the more visible the fisheye.

As the pavilion depth percentage rises above 48%, the diamond becomes darker in the center. The HRD lab (Hoge Raad vorr Diamant, Diamond High Council) in Antwerp, Belgium considers 41.5 to 45% to be a very good range for a round brilliant. The American Gem Society considers the ideal pavilion depth percentage of a round brilliant to fall between 42.2 and 43.8% of the average girdle diameter. The GIA has never listed the pavilion depth percentage on their diamond reports, but they teach it in their courses. However, they no longer specify recommended proportion ranges in their diamond grading courses because their research has found that there are many combinations of proportions that can provide attractive light return.

The only depth percentage listed on GIA reports has been the **total depth percentage**— the depth from the table to the culet, expressed as a percentage of the average girdle diameter in a round brilliant. According to the proportion standards of the HRD, very good round brilliants fall within a total depth percentage range of 55.5 to 63.9%. However, even if a diamond has an acceptable total depth, it could have a deep pavilion and low crown or vice versa. Consequently you can't determine if the pavilion of a diamond provides good light refraction just by reading a lab report that only lists the total depth percentage. Around the end of 2005, the GIA plans to add a cut grade to their diamond reports that will take into account light refraction from the pavilion.

Do not use the preceding depth percentage ranges to evaluate fancy shape diamonds. As I mentioned in Chapter 3, fancy shapes have different proportion and angle requirements than round brilliants.

Diamond cutters usually describe diamonds in terms of their angles instead of their depth percentages. The chart on the right converts the pavilion depth percentage into the **pavilion angle**—the angle between the girdle plane and the pavilion main facets (the large pavilion facets extending from the girdle to the culet on a brilliant-cut diamond; sometimes they are simply called pavilion facets, see fig. 4.1).

Pavilion Depth % Approximately	Pavilion Angle
40.0%	38.7°
40.5%	39.0°
41.0%	39.4°
41.5%	39.7°
42.0%	40.0°
42.5%	40.4°
43.0%	40.7°
43.5%	41.0°
44.0%	41.3°
44.5%	41.7°
45.0%	42.0°

Data from the GIA Diamond Grading Course

Crown

The crown (top of the diamond) usually plays the most important role in determining sparkle (technically called **scintillation**) and **fire** (a separation of white light into the colors of the rainbow, technically called **dispersion**).

If the crown is too thin, the diamond will have diminished sparkle and fire. When diamonds have the same table size, the shallower the crown, the smaller the **crown angle**—the angle between the girdle plane and the bezel facets (any of the four-sided, kite-shaped facets on the crown of a round brilliant-cut diamond, see fig 4.1).

When the crown is too high, the upper girdle and bezel facets will look crinkled. Flower-like patterns may be visible near the corners of the table (the large top facet) (fig. 4.8). Diamonds with very high crowns can have a lot of sparkle and fire; the problem is they tend to look small for their weight because too much weight is above the stone and not enough is spread across it.

Lay people can normally tell from the side view when a diamond is very thin or very high. Diamond professionals can also tell from the face-up view. Diamonds with very shallow crowns can still have good brilliance,

Fig 4.4 A well-proportioned diamond

Fig. 4.5 Diamond with a shallow pavilion and low crown

Fig. 4.6 Diamond with too much weight above the pavilion

Fig. 4.7 Diamond with a very thin crown and a deep pavilion.

Fig. 4.8 Face up view of a diamond with a high crown

Fig. 4.9 Diamond with excess weight and an uneven and very thick bruted girdle

so crown height does not have as much of an impact on price as pavilion depth. In fact, many princess- and radiant-cut diamonds have thin crowns.

Labs sometimes include the crown angle on their reports. The American Gem Society Laboratory considers a crown angle in the range of 33.7° to 35.8° to be ideal for standard round brilliant cut diamonds. The HRD Lab in Antwerp has a larger range of 30.7° to 37.7° for very good diamonds. The greater the angle, the higher the crown and vice versa. The GIA no longer uses angle and proportion measurements as the basis for grading cut.

A few labs also indicate the **crown height percentage**—distance between the girdle and table planes expressed as a percentage of the average girdle diameter. A crown height percentage range of 11 to 16% is classified as very good by the HRD lab in Antwerp.

Table

The size of the table (the large top facet) also plays a role in determining sparkle and fire. Table size is linked to the crown angle and crown height. When a diamond has a thin crown and steep crown angles, the table will be large.

The diamond reports of the major gem laboratories include the table percentage—a percentage of the average girdle diameter. For round brilliant cuts it is determined by dividing the largest table diameter by the average girdle diameter. For fancy shapes, it is calculated by dividing the width of the table by the width of the girdle.

Diamonds that the American Gem Society defines as ideal cuts have table sizes that range from 52.4 to 57.5%. Tables in this range can be spotted by the way their sides bow in (See figure 4.10). Europeans tend to like tables that are a little larger than this. The Antwerp HRD lab considers 53 to 66% to be a very good table size range. Diamonds with small tables tend to emphasize fire whereas diamonds with larger tables highlight more the brilliance of the diamond. Opinions differ as to what is the best balance between fire and brilliance.

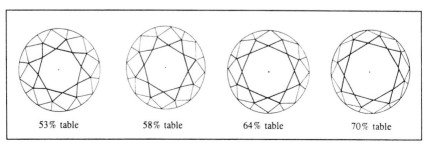

Fig 4.10 Four table sizes ranging from 53% to 70% of the girdle width. The 70% table is too large for good sparkle and fire. *Diagrams courtesy Gemological Institute of America*

Another but less exact way to estimate and compare table size is by the flash method, a term used by the GIA. Gently tilt a diamond back and forth under an overhead light source and note the flash of white light that reflects off the table. The larger the flash, the larger the table. Figure 4.11 shows this flash of white light on the six diamonds that are evaluated in the next chapter. The profile and normal face-up views are also shown.

Fig. 4.11 A reflective flash off the tables of the six diamonds studied in the next chapter. The 1st and 4th diamonds from the left have a 58% table, the 5th diamond has a 59% table. The exact table sizes of the other diamonds is not known, but the tables of the 2nd and 3rd diamonds are the largest. (2.5x)

Fig. 4.12 Same diamonds in the face-up position under normal lighting. From left to right: E I_1–2.20 cts ; G SI_2–0.70 cts; H VS_1–0.995 ct; I VS_2–1.00 ct; J SI_1–1.00 ct; L SI_3–1.41 cts

Fig. 4.13 The profile view helps explain why the "flat" second diamond is the least brilliant

Girdle

The girdle on a well-cut diamond protects it from chipping. If the girdle is too thick, it adds unnecessary weight to the stone and can sometimes detract from the appearance by causing a gray reflection in the stone. If the girdle is too thin, it may chip during setting or during everyday wear.

The girdle thickness is judged in relation to the size of the diamond and has grades ranging from extremely thin (a knife edge) to extremely thick (so thick that it is obvious to the unaided eye and may be difficult to set in jewelry).

The HRD lab in Antwerp classifies thin and medium girdles as very good. A round brilliant with a thin to medium or slightly thick girdle can receive an ideal cut grade of 0 by the American Gem Society Lab. It is normal and desirable for fancy-shape diamonds to be thick at the points. This helps protect the points from chipping.

There are three types of girdles:

◆ **Faceted**: with small facets (fig.4.13)
◆ **Bruted**: with a frosty, granular appearance (fig 4.14)
◆ **Polished**: with no facets, looking like a smooth continuous rim of glass going around the diamond

Fig. 4.13 Faceted girdle

Fig. 4.14 Bruted girdle

Bruted girdles should be smooth and precision cut. If they are rough, they can trap dirt, giving the girdle a dark look. Sometimes, girdles have fringes looking like whiskers and hairs. They are appropriately called **bearded girdles** and can lower the clarity grade of diamonds, especially those of high clarity.

Culet

The culet is the last facet polished on the diamond. It is there mainly to protect the bottom of the diamond from abrading and chipping. Not all diamonds have culets; in fact, most stones below 0.25 carat have none.

The American Gem Society Lab will grade the culet size as ideal if it is pointed, very small, small or medium sized. Old cuts typically have very large to extremely large culets. These diamonds are in high demand by antique dealers and are not viewed as low quality because of their very large culets.

Symmetry

Symmetry is a grading term for the exactness of shape and placement of facets. It is one of two subcategories of **finish**, which by GIA definition is the "quality of a diamond's polish, the condition of its girdle, and the precision of the cut." The other subcategory, polish, is discussed in the next section.

When gem laboratories assign a symmetry grade, they look for the following features:
◆ Out-of-round girdle outline
◆ Off-center culet
◆ Off-center table
◆ Tilted table, not parallel to the girdle plane
◆ Misshapen table that does not have sides of equal length and parallel opposing sides
◆ Wavy girdle that is not parallel to the table
◆ Girdle with unequal widths
◆ Pointing—facets fail to come to a point correctly.
◆ Misaligned crown and pavilion facets
◆ Similar facets of unequal size and shape
◆ Extra facets. (These only affect symmetry if they don't affect the clarity grade.)

The GIA grades symmetry with the grades Excellent (E), Very Good (VG), Good (G), Fair (F), and Poor (P). Grades of Excellent are rare. Most diamonds have some minor symmetry problems, but this does not normally affect their beauty. You should be more concerned about the pavilion proportions and overall brilliance of the diamond than its symmetry grade.

In order to highlight the symmetry of their diamonds, some stores and manufacturers show their diamonds through a special viewer that displays an optical effect of hearts and arrows. When a diamond is perfectly symmetrical, all of the hearts and arrows will look equally well formed (figure 4.14). The diamond must also be well-proportioned.

Fig 4.14 Hearts and arrows patterns. *Diamond, J Landau Inc; photo, Derse Studio.*

Polish

Polish refers to the overall condition of the facet surfaces of a polished diamond. It is a subcategory of finish. When labs evaluate polish, they examine the diamond under 10X magnification and look for surface blemishes that do not affect the clarity grade. Some of these characteristics are listed below:

◆ Polish lines (PL): Fine, tiny, parallel grooves caused by faceting
◆ Burn marks: Hazy surface areas caused by excessive heat
◆ Rough girdle (RG): An irregular, granular or pitted girdle surface
◆ Scratches (S): Thin white lines
◆ Pits: Minute indentations that look like tiny white dots
◆ Abrasions (Abr): Scraped spots or areas along the facet junctions or edges that have a white or fuzzy appearance
◆ Lizard skin: A bumpy polished surface that looks like goose bumps. (The term was coined by John Koivula in the late 1970's.)

The GIA uses the same grades for polish that it uses for symmetry. Diamonds that are well polished will produce sharper light reflections and look brighter than stones with an inadequate polish.

"Ideal-Cut" Diamonds

The term "ideal cut" is a marketing term used for excellent quality diamonds with proportions similar to those proposed by Marcel Tolkowsky, a mathematician and diamond cutter who is sometimes referred to as the "father" of the American brilliant cut.

The exact proportions of the "ideal-cut" vary depending on whom you talk to. However, now that the American Gem Society (AGS) has established a reputable gem laboratory that grades the cut of round diamonds, more and more trade professionals are accepting their criteria for defining the American "ideal cut." (Starting in 2005, they will also grade princess cuts). Nowadays, dealers usually send "ideal-cut" diamonds to the AGS laboratory so they can get the coveted cut grade of 0 on a grading report. Stones with a 0 cut grade sell at premiums of up to 15%.

Characteristics of the AGS American "ideal cut" are as follows:
◆ Average pavilion depth percentage of 42.2 to 43.8%
◆ Average crown angle of 33.7 to 35.8°
◆ Average table diameter of 52.4 to 57.5%
◆ Average girdle thickness of very thin, thin, medium or slightly thick
◆ Culet size of pointed, very small, small or medium

◆ Symmetry and polish grades of AGS 0, which means the polish and symmetry characteristics are extremely difficult to locate under 10-power magnification. The 0 grades are the GIA equivalent of excellent.

Fig. 4.15 An AGS-quality "ideal cut" diamond   **Fig. 4.16** Profile of the same "ideal cut"

"Ideal cuts" normally cost more than the average diamond because more weight is lost from the rough, and more skill and time are required to cut them. Figures 4.15 and 4.16 show the face-up and profile view of an "ideal cut" diamond with a 55% table. Compare the symmetry and precision of the cutting to that of many other diamonds and you'll understand why some people are willing to spend more for an "ideal cut."

Some cutters prefer diamonds with a slightly larger table than the AGS ideal cut and will cut them with the same degree of precision; the larger table makes the diamond appear a little bigger, yet it doesn't reduce brilliance. It's a matter of opinion which diamond proportions are best. There are ranges of acceptability and unacceptability, but even these can be debated.

The GIA has done considerable research using computer technology to measure diamond brilliance and fire. They have found that there are many combinations of proportions that can produce as much brilliance and fire as an American ideal cut. For this reason, they no longer use the Tolkowsky model to evaluate diamond cut in their diamond courses.

In short, American ideal cuts are beautiful diamonds, but there are other diamonds and cuts that will provide the same degree of beauty.

5

A Closer Look at Clarity

In Chapter 2, I briefly described inclusions, blemishes, and the clarity grades established by the GIA (Gemological Institute of America.). In this chapter, I'm going to discuss the grades in more detail and show you several views of six diamonds ranging in clarity from VS$_1$ to I$_1$. As a review, the clarity chart included in Chapter 2 is repeated below.

GIA CLARITY GRADES*	
* For trained graders using 10-power magnification and proper lighting	
Fl	**Flawless**, no blemishes or inclusions.
IF	**Internally flawless**, no inclusions and only insignificant blemishes.
VVS$_1$ & VVS$_2$	**Very, very slightly included**, minute inclusions that are difficult to see.
VS$_1$ & VS$_2$	**Very slightly included**, minor inclusions ranging from difficult to somewhat easy to see.
SI$_1$ & SI$_2$	**Slightly included**, noticeable inclusions that are easy (SI$_1$) or very easy (SI$_2$) to see.
I$_1$, I$_2$, & I$_3$ In Europe: P$_1$, P$_2$ & P$_3$	**Imperfect**, obvious inclusions that usually are eye-visible face up; in I$_3$, distinctions are based on the combined effect on durability, transparency, and brilliance.

Clarity Grades

Flawless   It's extremely rare that a diamond is flawless. Diamonds normally have at least a minor surface blemish.

According to the GIA Diamond Grading Course, a diamond can still qualify as Flawless if it has extra facets on the pavilion, naturals confined to the girdle, or internal graining that is not reflective, white or colored and that does not significantly affect transparency.

Internally Flawless (IF) Diamonds with no inclusions and only insignificant blemishes, such as tiny pits and scratches that are easily removed with repolishing can be classified internally flawless. It is unlikely that your jeweler has IF or Fl diamonds in stock. He might, however, be able to locate one for you.

VVS$_1$ & VVS$_2$ These diamonds have inclusions so small that the average person would not be able to find them under 10-power magnification. Even trained diamond graders may have to view the stone from several positions to find the inclusion. Some typical VVS flaws are pinpoints, minute hairline cracks, tiny bruises, bearding, and slight graining. Jewelers seldom keep VVS stones in stock, especially if they are one carat or more. To grade diamonds of VVS clarities, it's best to use a microscope, rather than just a 10-power loupe.

VS$_1$ A lay person would have a hard time finding the very small crystals, clouds, cracks (feathers) or pinpoints that characterize this grade. Sometimes, he or she may not be able to find them under ten-power magnification. Some stores keep large VS$_1$ diamonds in stock, but if they have a wide selection of them, be suspicious of over grading because they're not readily available in large quantities.

VS$_2$ Diamonds with this classification have the same types of inclusions as VS$_1$ stones but the inclusions are either more numerous, larger or easier to see.

SI$_1$ Even though this is the seventh clarity grade from the top, this is still an excellent grade. If you look at an SI$_1$ stone face-up with the unaided eye, you won't see any inclusions. If you look at it with 10-power magnification, you'll notice small cracks (feathers), clouds or crystals.

SI$_2$ Sometimes you can see the inclusions of these stones through the pavilion (bottom) of the stone with the naked eye, but normally, the inclusions are not visible through the crown. An exception to this would be with large diamonds and with emerald-cut diamonds. As the GIA points out in their diamond grading course, inclusions in such diamonds are easier to see because of their larger facets. The inclusions of the SI grades generally do not affect the durability of the stone.

SI$_3$ An intermediary grade between I$_1$ and SI$_2$, which was first introduced on reports by the EGL (European Gem Laboratory). It is also used by PGS (Professional Gem Sciences) and is seen on trade price lists. The GIA, IGI (International Gemological Institute) and AGS (American Gem Society) labs do not use the SI$_3$ grade on their reports; and to my knowledge, none of the other major laboratories listed in Chapter 11 use it either.

I$_1$ (P$_1$) The inclusions of this grade are obvious at 10-power magnification, but in small brilliant-cut diamonds, they are barely visible to the unaided eye through the crown. This can be a good clarity grade choice for people on a limited budget. Often a well-cut I$_1$ looks better than a poorly cut SI diamond.

I$_2$ (P$_2$) The inclusions are often easily visible to the unaided eye and may affect the beauty and durability of the diamond. This grade is frequently used in discount jewelry.

I$_3$ (P$_3$) These diamonds frequently look shattered, as if they'd been hammered. Sometimes they have no cracks, but they're so filled with crystal inclusions that they have a muddy gray or whitish look. An I$_3$ grade would be unacceptable to someone interested in a brilliant and transparent diamond.

Clarity grading requires more than identification of diamond inclusions. An overall visual impression must be formed of the diamond with and without 10-power magnification, and the grading conditions must be considered. Keep in mind the following:

◆ Each grade represents a range of quality. Consequently, diamonds of the same clarity grade are not always equally desirable. That's why it is important to visually examine stones instead of just relying on grades when making your choice. In some cases, a high I$_1$ diamond can look better than a low SI$_2$ stone when set.

◆ Prongs and settings can hide flaws. Consequently, only approximate clarity grades can be assigned to diamonds set in jewelry. If you're interested in a stone with a high clarity, it may be best for you to buy a loose stone and have it set.

◆ Diamonds must be clean for accurate grading. Dirt and dust can look like inclusions.

◆ Big inclusions generally lower grades more than small ones. Usually one or two of the largest inclusions establish the clarity grade.

◆ The type of inclusion can have a dramatic effect on the grade. For example, a small feather (crack) will tend to lower a grade more than a pinpoint inclusion.

◆ Dark inclusions tend to lower grades more than colorless and white inclusions. Sometimes, however, white inclusions stand out more than black ones due to their position.

◆ Inclusions under the table (in the center) of the diamond tend to lower grades more than those near the girdle (around the edges).

Diamond Clarity Examples

A month before I started writing this book, I photographed six diamonds, each of a different clarity ranging from VS_1 to I_1. They were selected at random and then photographed from different angles both through the lens of a microscope and through a camera lens. No special photographic lights were used. The photos were shot with either the lighting on the microscope or with ordinary incandescent desk lamps or with a combination of the two types of lighting. In some of the captions you will see the term **darkfield illumination.** This means the light is coming from the side against a black background in the microscope. It highlights the flaws and usually makes the diamond look worse than under normal lighting. The overhead lighting view most closely approximates the view through a loupe. In this view, the light is above the stone.

I photographed the diamonds in this manner in order to give you a fuller understanding of the clarity grades than what you would get from just seeing single face-up photos of the diamonds. Three of the diamonds happened to come with GIA grading reports and three had EGL mini certificates (shortened version of a full grading report).

With the exception of the grading and proportion information taken from the lab documents, all comments about the diamonds are based on my opinion. Other qualified trade professionals may disagree with some of my statements. I will be giving you the perspective of a gemologist with experience in the wholesale diamond trade.

Diamond 1: VS₁ , H color, EGL LA, 0.995 ct

Fig. 5.1 VS₁, 7x, darkfield illumination

Fig. 5.2 VS₁, 7x, overhead lighting

Fig. 5.3 (VS₁) Clouds, which are only visible in the pavilion view and a tiny crystal. The inclusions are reflected so they appear doubled.

Fig. 5.4 (VS₁) Profile view, overhead lighting.

Diamond 2: VS₂ , I color, GIA, 1.00 ct; 63.3% depth; 58% table; medium to slightly thick faceted girdle; no culet, good polish, good symmetry

Fig. 5.5 VS₂, darkfield and overhead lighting

Fig. 5.6 VS₂, 7x, overhead lighting

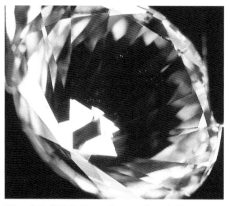

Fig. 5.7 (VS₂) Crystal near the girdle at one o'clock position and pinpoints. Darkfield light.

Fig. 5.8 (VS₂) Profile view, overhead lighting

Fig. 5.9 (VS₂) Indented naturals and an extra facet that was considered a clarity feature by the lab. This is an ideal set of "birthmarks" for a diamond. They are not visible from the top view and they distinguish the stone from all other diamonds.

Diamond 3: SI₁, J color, GIA, 1.00 ct; 65.4% depth; 59% table; thin to thick faceted girdle; no culet, good polish, good symmetry

Fig. 5.10 SI₁, 8x, darkfield illumination

Fig. 5.11 SI₁, 8x , overhead lighting

Fig 5.12 (SI₁) Feather, pinpoints and tiny crystals at 9 o'clock position, small crystal and pinpoint just above the culet, darkfield lighting

Fig. 5.13 (SI₁) profile view, overhead lighting

Diamond 4: SI₂, G color, EGL LA, 0.701 ct

Fig. 5.14 SI₂, 7x, darkfield illumination

Fig. 5.15 SI₂, 7x , overhead lighting

Fig. 5.16 SI₂, 7x, darkfield & overhead light

Fig. 5.17 (SI₂), profile view

Diamond 5: SI₃, L color, EGL LA, 1.406 cts

Fig. 5.18 SI₃, 7x, darkfield illumination

Fig. 5.19 SI₃, 7x, overhead lighting

Fig. 5.20 SI₃, darkfield and overhead lighting

Fig. 5.21 (SI₃) profile view

Fig. 5.22 (SI₃) Bearded girdle and natural. Repolishing could improve the girdle.

Fig. 5.23 SI₃, 17x, Inclusions that look black with overhead lighting as in figure 5.19

Diamond 6: I₁ , E color, GIA, 2.20 ct; 61.1% depth; 58% table; medium to thick faceted girdle; no culet, good polish, fair symmetry

Fig. 5.24 I₁, 6x, darkfield illumination

Fig. 5.25 I₁, 6x, overhead lighting

Fig. 5.26 I₁, darkfield and overhead lighting

Fig. 5.27 (I₁) profile view

Fig. 5.28 I₁, darkfield illumination

Fig. 5.29 I₁, darkfield illumination

Only one of the preceding diamonds would I advise people not to buy, and that is the 0.701 ct, SI_2, G color diamond. It has a good color grade and a respectable clarity grade, but it looks dull and dark, especially when compared to the other diamonds (fig. 5.30). This is because the crown and pavilion are not well proportioned.

Fig. 5.30 Face-up views of the six diamonds. Left to right: I_1, SI_3, SI_2. SI_1, VS_2, and VS_1 (actual size). Their inclusions are not noticeable but the lower brilliance of the SI_2 diamond is apparent.

By contrast, the diamond with the lowest color grade, the 1.41 ct, SI_3, L color stone, is bright and sparkly. In my opinion, color is a matter of personal preference. For example, a blouse with a faint yellow color is not inferior to one that is white. In the diamond world, however, colorless diamonds are more rare and in higher demand than diamonds with yellowish tints. Consequently, colorless diamonds are higher-priced. If this diamond were D color, it would probably cost 75% more, all other factors being equal. When you have a strict budget, color can be a good factor on which to compromise.

The 2.20 carat, I_1, E color diamond would be appropriate for someone more interested in the size and color grade. A person could buy this stone for about one-third the price of an IF or VVS_1 diamond of the same color grade, all other factors being equal, or for about half the price of a VS_2 diamond. Under normal lighting this is an impressive diamond, and its inclusions are small enough that they are not visible to the naked eye.

On the subject of lighting, you should not restrict your view of diamonds under magnification to darkfield illumination. Turn on the overhead microscope light so that you can see the brilliance of the diamond magnified. Darkfield lighting masks brilliance, exaggerates flaws and is seldom used by dealers in the process of buying and selling gems. They normally use loupes, and the light is above and/or to the side of the diamond over a white background. Darkfield illumination is most helpful for detecting treatments and imitation diamonds, and for grading clarities of VVS and above.

Sometimes inclusions look white under darkfield illumination, but black when you look at them with a loupe or under the microscope fluorescent lamp. Dark inclusions, especially those in the center of the table, have a greater impact on the clarity grade than those that are white. This is another reason to look at diamonds with overhead lighting.

When purchasing diamonds, you should compare them next to other diamonds. Move the stones when judging brilliance. The apparent brightness of each diamond can change depending on the distance of the diamonds from the lamp and their position in the tray. A larger view of these six diamonds is shown in the previous chapter. However, they are arranged in the order of their descending color grades instead of their ascending order of clarity.

Diamonds with clarity grades lower than I_1 are not often sent to gem labs for grading. Some examples of I_2 and I_3 grades are shown below and on the next page.

Fig. 5.31 I_2

Fig. 5.32 I_2

Fig. 5.33 I_2

Fig. 5.34 I_2

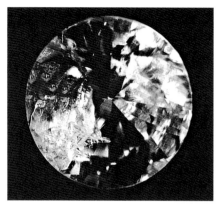

Fig.5.35 I₃,

Fig. 5.36 I₃

6

Fluorescence

When a Burma ruby is placed under ultraviolet (UV) light, it typically will have a beautiful red or red-orange glow. This glow is called **fluorescence**, which is the emission of visible light by a material when it's stimulated by ultraviolet light, x-rays or other forms of radiation. The term "fluorescence" comes from the mineral fluorite (calcium fluoride), which is noted for displaying an array of intense fluorescent colors. Like rubies, many diamonds exhibit this characteristic.

It's helpful to understand the basic principles of light in order to understand fluorescence. The various types of light are defined in terms of wavelengths, which are measured in nanometers (one millionth of a millimeter, abbreviated nm). See graph below:

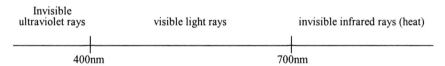

The light that the human eye can see falls approximately between 400nm and 700nm. These are the same wavelengths as the colors of the rainbow which start from violet at 400nm and extend to red at 700nm.

Light with wavelengths longer than approximately 700 nm is called **infrared light**. We can't see this light, but we can feel it as heat.

Light with wavelengths shorter than 400nm is called **ultraviolet light**. Even though we can't see or feel this light, it can still have an effect on us. For example, it can cause our skin to sunburn and tan.

Scientists divide the wavelength range of ultraviolet light into the four sections shown on the graph below.

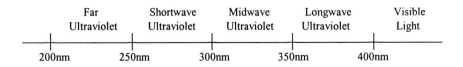

Longwave UV light is known among hobbyists as "black light." It's present in sunlight and causes some minerals to fluoresce as well as other items such as teeth, fingernails, and some paints, fabric and ink. Longwave UV light doesn't seem to have a negative effect on the skin or body.

Midwave UV light is also present in sunlight and induces fluorescence in some minerals. When its wavelengths are shorter than 310nm, it helps the body absorb vitamin D and it causes the skin to tan or burn, depending on th e length of exposure.

Shortwave UV light is absorbed by the earth's atmosphere, so it is not present in sunlight. Shortwave UV lamps are especially effective in stimulating mineral fluorescence and are widely used by hobbyists as well as gemologists. When using these lamps, one must avoid overexposure because this light can also cause sunburn.

Far UV light extends from about 20 nm to 250nm. Gemologists and mineralogists are not concerned with this light because air absorbs it. Research on far UV light must be conducted in a vacuum. X-rays fall below far UV light and have wavelengths between .01 and 10–20 nanometers.

Besides being used for gem and mineral identification, UV light has a variety of practical applications, which include:

◆ Treatment of skin disorders and eye problems

◆ Detection of counterfeit bills

◆ Destruction of bacteria, sterilization

◆ Study and analysis of cell cultures and biological samples

◆ Water purification

◆ Detection of metal stress and cracks in aerospace and defense industries

◆ Quality control in the agricultural industries. Stored food, for example, can be examined for signs of rodent urine, which fluoresces.

(The material in the preceding section is primarily based on information from a chapter entitled "The Magic of Ultraviolet Light" by Thomas Warren in the book *Ultraviolet Light and Fluorescent Minerals*. Warren, is the founder and president of Ultra-Violet Products, Inc.)

Diamond Fluorescence

When diamonds fluoresce under UV light, they usually display a blue color, but they may also look violet, green, yellow, orange, red or white; or they may show a combination of colors. The fluorescence is often patchy or in bands. Sometimes the diamonds continue to glow after the UV light is turned off. This continued emission of visible light after the light source is removed is called **phosphorescence**.

Diamonds with blue fluorescence typically have a yellow-green phosphorescence, which is a positive test for diamond. If the diamond is then heated, it will glow blue again, and this effect is called **thermo-phosphorescence**. Under X-rays, diamond will usually have a uniform bluish white glow. Cathode radiation (electron radiation) gives the most brilliant fluorescent effects and causes some diamonds to glow different colors on different faces. (from Eric Bruton's *Diamonds).*

Lab reports usually indicate the strength and color of a diamond's fluorescence to longwave UV light. The description is not a grade; it is just a further means of identifying the diamond. The GIA Gem Trade Laboratory categorizes the levels of strength as "none," "faint," "medium," "strong," or "very strong,"

Not all labs use the same categories. The AGS (American Gem Society) Laboratories has four categories: "negligible," "medium," "strong" and "very strong."

The following conditions may influence the observed fluorescence reactions:

◆ The distance of the UV lamp to the gemstone being examined. The closer the lamp is to a diamond, the stronger the reaction may be.

◆ The darkness of the room in which the stone is viewed.

◆ The strength of the fluorescence. For weak fluorescence reactions, it is sometimes difficult to accurately see and describe the fluorescence color. Use of a reference of known fluorescence color can help the observer in such situations.

◆ The type of lamp used. Both the UV lamp and the filters in the lamps can vary from one manufacturer to another. In addition, both the lamp and the filters can degrade over time, and this may influence observed fluorescence reactions.

What Causes Diamond Fluorescence?

Trace elements and irregularities in the atomic structure of a mineral can cause both gem color and fluorescence. Even though the chemical formula for diamond consists only of carbon, it can have traces of other elements such as nitrogen, aluminum and boron. When nitrogen and aluminum substitute together for carbon atoms, blue fluorescence can result. Single nitrogen atoms coupled with a carbon vacancy can cause yellow fluorescence. Two nitrogen atoms associated with crystal irregularities due to radiation damage can activate greenish-yellow fluorescence.

The information in the preceding paragraph is from pages 194 and 195 of *Ultraviolet Light and Fluorescent Minerals,* in a chapter entitled "Activators in Fluorescent Minerals." It's written by Earl R. Verbeek, a research geologist with the U.S. Geological Survey.

Is Ultraviolet Lighting the Same as Fluorescent Lighting?

No , it's not the same. Ultraviolet lamps emit mostly UV light, whereas fluorescent lamps emit mostly visible light. Even though both types of lamps are made from glass tubes with cathodes inserted at both ends, the fluorescent tube is coated with a phosphor on the inside walls that absorbs UV light and re-emits it as visible light.

A short-wave UV lamp, on the other hand, has a clear tube and a filter that blocks the passage of visible light and allows shortwave UV light to pass through. The primary emissions of shortwave UV lights are typically about 254 to 255 nanometers.

Longwave UV lamps use tubes with a longwave-emitting phosphor coating on the inside. These tubes are similar in appearance and construction to fluorescent tubes, but the phosphor coating is designed to emit longwave UV light rather than visible light. The primary emissions of longwave UV lamps are at about 365 to 366 nanometers. For more information, see pages 12–21 of *Ultraviolet Light and Fluorescent Minerals.*

Are Fluorescent Diamonds Undesirable?

It seems common sense that a diamond's beauty should be judged on its appearance in normal light, not under a longwave UV lamp. Nevertheless many consumers have been told to reject diamonds solely on the basis of a lab report stating that the diamond fluoresces under UV light. As a result, more and more people are starting to believe that fluorescent diamonds are undesirable. In fact, some consumers who chose a diamond for its beauty are now wondering if it's defective just because their lab report states that it has medium or strong fluorescence in UV light.

I used to work full time in the diamond industry, and I had the opportunity to visit the offices of many diamond dealers in the Los Angeles diamond district. I would observe how they examined diamonds during transactions. Never did I see a dealer place a diamond under a UV light and examine the stone's fluorescence in order to determine if he wanted to buy it. Fluorescence was not an issue. What mattered was quality and the overall life of the diamond.

When I sorted parcels of diamonds, I looked at each stone with a loupe under fluorescent and diamond grading light, but never under UV light. If a diamond was milky white, it was obvious when I looked at it, and the diamond was placed in a rejection pile. If the diamond was hazy, it was downgraded. Transparency was important, but that quality was determined by examining the stone under normal lighting.

Since diamond grading reports and the Internet are being used more now in the purchase of jewelry, fluorescence has become a subject of concern for consumers. They read a lot of conflicting information on the Internet and wonder what to believe:

I did a search of "diamond fluorescence" on the Internet, and found four main viewpoints:

1. A few sites say to avoid diamonds with fluorescence because they claim it makes diamonds look, oily, hazy or milky white, and consequently, lowers their price. They don't mention the fact that a lot of highly transparent diamonds are fluorescent, but the sites may indicate that they have non-fluorescent diamonds for sale.

2. Several sites say fluorescence is bad for D, E & F color diamonds, especially if the fluorescence is medium to very strong. Some say it's also bad for those of G & H color. According to these sites, fluorescence makes high color diamonds look oily, hazy or cloudy. If this were true, why wouldn't it also decrease the transparency of lower color diamonds?

3. Several sites say blue fluorescence is desirable for diamonds with a color grade lower than I or J because it can make them look whiter in sunlight, particularly when it's strong. As a result, a premium may be charged depending on the degree of fluorescence. While it's true that blue fluorescence may cancel out some of the yellow in yellowish diamonds when they are viewed face up in sunlight, that doesn't warrant a surcharge, especially when there are other sellers telling customers to avoid fluorescent diamonds.

4   A few sites promote fluorescence because it may make slightly yellowish diamonds look whiter in sunlight and/or because diamonds look pretty when they fluoresce under ultraviolet light.

On the front cover of the winter 1997 issue of *Gems and Gemology* is a photograph of a well-matched, transparent diamond necklace and an earring by Harry Winston. Half the necklace and one earring are shown under normal lighting conditions; the other half and the same earring are shown under longwave ultraviolet light. (See figure 6.1 and the inside back cover.) Even though the diamonds have a range of fluorescent strengths, they have a uniform attractive appearance under normal lighting conditions.

The Harry Winston necklace is not an unusual example. Photographs of important diamond pieces viewed under fluorescent lighting used to be taken for identification purposes. If someone made a copy of the piece, it was easy to detect the copy by comparing it with the pattern of diamond fluorescence in the original piece.

GEMS & GEMOLOGY

VOLUME XXXIII   WINTER 1997

THE QUARTERLY JOURNAL OF THE GEMOLOGICAL INSTITUTE OF AMERICA

Fig. 6.1 Half the necklace and one earring in this composite photo are shown under normal lighting conditions (left), and the other half of the necklace and the same earring are shown as they appear under a long-wave ultraviolet lamp (right). Even though diamonds in a range of fluorescent strengths are placed next to diamonds with faint or no fluorescence (the darkest stones), the jewelry has a uniform overall appearance under normal lighting conditions. (See inside back cover for color photo.) *Jewelry courtesy Harry Winston, Inc.; photos by Harold & Erica Van Pelt. Photo reprinted with permission from the Gemological Institute of America.*

The Hope Diamond, a famous blue diamond on display at the Smithsonian Institution in Washington D.C., is noted for its unusual strong red fluorescence. John S. White, former curator-in-charge of gems & minerals, says the Hope Diamond not only fluoresces red like a hot coal but also phosphoresces for several minutes once the light source has been turned off. He describes its transparency as excellent. This is a good example of how fluorescence does not detract from the beauty of a diamond.

If someone were to present us with the Hope diamond, would we turn it down just because it is strongly fluorescent? Would it deserve to be discounted?

If someone offered us a Harry Winston necklace with D, E & F color diamonds of varying degrees of fluorescence, would we be disappointed? Should the diamonds be discounted because of their fluorescence?

If we wouldn't reject these diamonds, than why should we reject any other fluorescent diamond simply because sites on the Internet suggest they are undesirable?

The power of the written word is sometimes amazing. In 1829, Sir Walter Scott published his novel *Anne of Gerstein*. In it, one of the characters wore a gorgeous opal that would change color depending on her mood. One day when a few drops of holy water were sprinkled on the opal, she fainted and died shortly thereafter. Convinced that this meant opals were unlucky, readers stopped buying the gem. Within a year of the novel's publication, the opal market had crashed and prices were down about 50 per cent. Even today, there are a few people who think opals bring bad luck even though it was considered a lucky gemstone prior to 1829.

My Advice Regarding Diamond Fluorescence

The preceding section was entitled, "Are fluorescent diamonds undesirable?" In my opinion, the answer is no. A diamond with fluorescence can be just as attractive as one with none. When we buy a diamond, we're buying a gemstone, not a lab report; we should pay more attention to how the diamond looks under normal lighting than to its UV fluorescence description on the report

Finding a diamond in a desired size, shape, color, quality and price range is a challenge. Why make the process more difficult by ruling out attractive transparent diamonds that happen to be fluorescent? If you find a good-quality diamond you like at the right price, consider buying it whether or not it's fluorescent. Here is some additional advice:

◆ If a seller offers a discount because a diamond is fluorescent, accept the discount.

◆ If a seller asks for a premium because a diamond has blue fluorescence, don't pay it. There are plenty of other sellers who don't charge extra for such diamonds. If the fluorescence has an unusual color, the premium may be warranted. Collectors of fluorescent gems want them.

◆ View diamonds under various types of normal lighting—fluorescent lamps, daylight, light bulbs. If you select diamonds that look good in the light sources under which they will be worn, it won't matter what their color or fluorescence strength is under UV light.

◆ If a diamond has medium to very strong blue fluorescence, be glad because this is a good indication that the diamond is natural and not synthetic. (See Chapter 7 on synthetic diamonds for more information.)

◆ Base your choice of diamond on its actual appearance, rather than on the description of its fluorescence on a lab report.

Two Good Sources of Information on Diamond Fluorescence

◆ The book *Ultraviolet Light and Fluorescent Minerals* by Thomas S. Warren, Sterling Gleason, Richard C. Bostwick and Earl R. Verbeek

◆ The article "A Contribution to Understanding the Effect of Blue Fluorescence on the Appearance of Diamonds" by Thomas Moses, Ilene Reinitz, Mary Johnson, John King, and James Shigley in the winter 1997 issue of *Gems & Gemology*.

7

Synthetic Diamonds

Synthetic (man-made) diamonds were first produced in the early 1950's for industrial purposes, but it's only recently that they've become commercially available for use in jewelry. The lab-grown diamonds I saw on sale at the 2004 Tucson Gem Show were beautiful. Their prices ranged from around $2000 to several thousand dollars per carat.

In 2004, synthetic diamonds made from the carbon remains of family members and pets were advertised on the Internet for $13,999 in sizes from 0.90–0.99 carat. The prices went as low as $2499 for sizes from 0.20–0.29 carat for a dead-person-turned-diamond. These diamonds had been introduced to the market in 2002 for prices as high as $20,000.

What are Synthetic Diamonds?

Synthetic diamonds are diamonds made in a laboratory that have essentially the same chemical composition and crystal structure as natural diamonds. Their physical and optical properties are almost the same as natural diamonds.

Cubic zirconia (CZ) is not synthetic diamond. It's a diamond imitation (termed simulant in the trade) because it has a different chemical composition than a diamond. Some CZ's are marketed in stores and on the Internet as synthetic diamonds, but this is considered an unethical trade practice. CZ's are not man-made diamonds; they're fake diamonds.

Marketers of synthetic diamonds usually identify their diamonds with terms such as "lab grown," "lab-created," "created," and "man-made;" whereas gemologists and natural stone dealers usually refer to them as synthetic diamonds. A few sellers call them "cultured diamonds" and compare them to cultured pearls. This is misleading advertising. The next section will explain why.

How Does Growing Diamonds Differ from Culturing Pearls?

There are two basic types of lab-created diamonds—HPHT synthetic diamonds (those grown under high pressures and high temperatures) and CVD synthetic diamonds (those produced using chemical vapor deposition techniques).

HPHT created diamonds are grown by placing a carbon-containing solid in the center of a special pressure chamber and surrounding it with a metal flux such as iron or nickel (a flux is a solid material that dissolves other materials when melted). After applying extremely high pressure and high temperatures under controlled conditions, carbon is dissolved in the molten flux. The carbon atoms move to tiny diamond seed crystals near the chamber walls and begin to grow. Within a few days, new synthetic diamond crystals suitable for faceting are formed.

CVD synthetic diamonds are produced at low pressures by placing minute synthetic diamond seed crystals in an environment with carbon-containing gases. The gas molecules are broken apart during decomposition and carbon atoms are deposited on the "seeds," causing them to grow into lab-created diamond crystals.

Cultured pearls are not grown in laboratories. They grow in oysters or mussels after man implants a shell bead or a piece of tissue from the mollusk in them. The nacre (pearl coating) isn't created in a laboratory. It's secreted by the mollusk around the irritant. Cultured pearls take a few months to a couple of years to form, not just a few days like synthetics.

Some sellers are telling customers that man-made diamonds are grown just like cultured pearls. Besides being misleading, this is unfair to the pearl industry. A cultured pearl is a much more natural product than a lab-created diamond.

What's the Biggest Disadvantage of Synthetic Gems?

The biggest drawback is that synthetic gemstones may not hold their value. When synthetic rubies were first produced around 1890, they cost about as much as natural rubies. Today one of those pretty, clear red, lab-created rubies in a carat size can be bought for just a couple of dollars, unless it's mounted in antique jewelry, where the value of the whole piece may be worth more than the sum of the parts. However, a natural one-carat ruby of fine quality could be worth over $2500.

A more recent example is hydrothermal synthetic emerald, the type that most closely approximates natural emerald. It was retailing for up to $1000 a carat at the beginning of the 1990's, but by the end of the decade, you could find this lab-grown emerald retailing for as low as $20 per carat at public gem shows.

Up until now, very few synthetic diamonds have been on the market because of the high costs involved in producing them. Prices are now coming down substantially. The diamonds made from the remains of dead people are one example. In just two years, the larger stones have dropped a few thousand dollars. During the same period, natural diamond prices have either remained the same or gone up. In fact, some dealers are complaining about how difficult it is to find high quality diamond rough and how they have to pay more than they can afford.

In general, synthetics should be priced appreciably lower than natural stones, even if they may be more perfect than the naturals. This is not only because they are manmade, but also because in theory, at least, the supply is virtually limitless.

When new synthetics first appear they tend to be quite expensive, given that they are not natural. With time, they all experience a drop in price as production costs and other factors such as competition from multiple labs make this possible or necessary. Consequently, the prices of lab-created diamonds will continue to drop, probably to a level where they become a more affordable option. Meanwhile, if you're about to buy a diamond and you'd like it to retain its value, select an untreated diamond of natural origin, one that has been mined in the earth.

Detecting Synthetic Diamonds

When cubic zirconia (CZ) entered the market in the 1970's, many people were concerned that it would ruin the diamond market because of its close resemblance to diamond. After jewelers learned how CZ differed from diamond, they were able to distinguish the two stones visually. The process of detecting CZ's was further aided by the development of the thermal diamond tester.

In the late 1990's, there was alarm over the introduction of synthetic moissanite (another diamond imitation) because it was able to fool diamond testers and jewelers. But jewelers eventually learned how to visually detect it. Moissanite detectors were also developed.

Even though most jewelers are not currently able to distinguish synthetic diamonds from those that are natural, the major gem laboratories are able to identify all lab-grown diamonds since synthetics don't have all of the same physical and optical properties as natural stones. This is because they are not formed in exactly the same way.

Researchers and gem laboratories are sharing their findings with trade members, so more and more jewelers will be able to detect man-made diamonds. The manufacturers of lab-grown diamonds have been very cooperative and generous in providing samples of their products to gem labs for analysis.

DeBeers has already developed three diamond instruments that can separate natural from synthetic yellow, brown, blue, orange and colorless to near-colorless diamonds. They are working on developing lower priced synthetic diamond testers.

A high percentage of natural and synthetic diamonds can be distinguished from each other just by observing their fluorescence under a UV lamp. Some of the main differences are:

◆ **Natural diamonds usually fluoresce stronger to LW (longwave) than to SW (shortwave) light, whereas most synthetics fluoresce stronger to SW.** However, some synthetic diamonds that have undergone high temperature and high-pressure color treatment fluoresce stronger to LW than to SW.

◆ **Blue is the most common LW fluorescent color of colorless and yellow natural diamonds.** The fluorescent colors of HPHT synthetic yellow to colorless diamonds are normally greenish yellow to chalky yellow, although on rare occasions pale bluish white colors have been noted. CVD man-made diamonds typically have an orange to orange-yellow or yellow-green UV fluorescence.

If you have a yellow, colorless, or near colorless diamond with medium to very strong blue UV fluorescence, it's a natural diamond.

◆ **The distribution of UV fluorescence in natural diamonds tends to be more even than in synthetic diamonds.** Some HPHT synthetic diamonds have characteristic cross and hour-glass fluorescence patterns, whereas CVD diamonds often display straight groove-like parallel lines under UV light that are difficult to see without magnification and strong short wave UV light like that used in DeBeers Diamond View Instrument.

◆ **Synthetic colorless to blue diamonds normally glow (phosphoresce) longer under SW UV than natural diamonds** after the UV light is switched off. In fact, some synthetic diamonds continue to glow for several minutes to hours in the dark. Scottish gemologist Alan Hodgkinson reports observing a DeBeer's synthetic blue diamond that phosphoresces for several days, though the phosphorescence is very weak after about an hour. By contrast, the glow of natural diamonds typically lasts less than 30 seconds, although exceptions are encountered as with the famous Cullinan diamonds.

See Tables 7.1 and 7.2 for more detailed information on the fluorescence and phosphorescence of diamonds.

UV lamps are more affordable than most of the other instruments used by labs to detect synthetic diamonds. Small hand-held LW UV lamps are available for as low as US$25. You can find small SW UV lamps for as low as US$50. As the wattage or strength of the light goes up, so does the price. Appraisers can buy a decent LW/SW lamp for less than $300. Major labs pay more for stronger and higher-quality lamps.

Table 7.1

Description of diamond	Intensity & color of fluorescence under longwave UV lamp	Intensity & color of fluorescence under shortwave UV lamp
Natural colorless to near colorless	occasionally none visible; weak to very strong blue or sometimes yellow or orange	none visible or weak to strong blue or sometimes yellow or orange
Synthetic colorless to near colorless	HPHT: none visible; CVD: usually weak yellow or orange	HPHT: weak to strong yellow, green-yellow or orange-yellow; CVD: very weak to strong orange-yellow or yellow- green
Natural yellow	sometimes none; otherwise weak to very strong blue or yellow; sometimes orange, rarely green	sometimes none; other-wise weak to strong blue or yellow; sometimes orange; occasionally green
Irradiated & HPHT-treated yellow	weak to strong yellow to green	weak to strong yellow to green
HPHT synthetic yellow	occasionally none; usually weak to strong yellow or yellow-green	usually weak to strong yellow to yellow-green,
Irradiated HPHT synthetic pink/purple	weak to strong reddish or pinkish orange	medium to very strong reddish or pinkish orange
Natural blue	usually none; rare: weak to moderate orange-red	usually none; occasionally yellowish to bluish white, rare: weak to moderate orange to orange-red
Synthetic blue	usually none visible, occasionally weak grayish blue or brownish orange	weak to moderate yellow, green-yellow, grayish blue, or brownish orange

The above table was based on information in "A Chart for the Separation of Natural and Synthetic Diamonds" by the GIA,.*The MicroWorld of Diamonds* by John Koivula, articles in *Gems & Gemology,* and personal communication with Branko Deljanin & Sharrie Woodring, EGL USA research and Alan Hodgkinson.

Table 7.2

Description of diamond	Phosphorescence	Distribution of UV fluorescence (best seen under magnification)
Natural colorless or near colorless	rarely weak yellow (LW & SW) lasting 30 seconds or less	usually even, but sometimes uneven with concentric bands of octahedral growth
Synthetic colorless	weak to strong yellow, greenish yellow, or greenish blue (SW) lasting 60 seconds or more	HPHT synthetic: sometimes uneven distribution, often with a square or octagon plus a cross-shaped growth pattern through the crown and/ or an hourglass pattern from the side. CVD: even to barely visible curved growth striations (best seen under the DeBeers Diamond View instrument)
Natural yellow	occasionally weak to moderate yellow (LW & SW) usually less than 15 seconds	usually even, rarely uneven; may show blue and yellow fluorescent patches of color
Irradiated & HPHT **treated yellow**	very weak greenish yellow (SW), less than 15 seconds	
HPHT synthetic yellow	usually none, sometimes weak yellow or greenish yellow lasting several seconds	uneven distribution like colorless synthetic diamonds
Irradiated, HPHT **synthetic pink/purple**	usually none,	usually even
Natural blue	very rarely bluish white to LW and almost always bluish white to SW; rarely weak to moderate, yellow orange to orange red lasting less than 15 seconds	usually even
Synthetic blue	moderate to strong yellow to SW lasting 30–60 seconds or as long as an hour	uneven distribution like colorless synthetic diamonds

The above table was based on information in "A Chart for the Separation of Natural and Synthetic Diamonds" by the GIA,.*The MicroWorld of Diamonds* by John Koivula, articles in *Gems & Gemology,* and personal communication with Branko Deljanin & Sharrie Woodring, EGL USA Research and Alan Hodgkinson..

Here are a few tips for judging the UV fluorescence of diamonds:

◆ View the diamond(s) against a black background.

◆ View the diamonds in a totally dark room.

◆ Allow your eyes to adjust to the darkness so very weak reactions can be observed.

◆ Place the UV lamp as close to the diamond(s) as possible.

◆ Avoid looking at the fluorescent UV light tube.

◆ It's good to wear protective eye wear when viewing diamonds under UV lamps, especially under shortwave UV. The longer the viewing time the more advisable it is.

◆ For best results, it's helpful to have comparison stones when judging single stones. Fluorescence and phosphorescence tests can also be effectively used on parcels of diamonds to quickly sort out diamonds that are obviously natural or synthetic. Questionable diamonds can undergo further testing.

HPHT synthetic diamonds often have characteristic inclusions, which allow them to be identified under magnification, but this is more difficult than UV fluorescence tests, especially when the stones are of high clarity.

Major gem laboratories use a combination of tests along with high-tech, expensive equipment like spectrometers to detect impurities in the UV-Visible-Near-infrared spectra of synthetic diamonds. They also have more experience identifying synthetic diamonds. Therefore, when purchasing an expensive diamond, it's advisable to get a lab report stating that the diamond is of natural origin. For more information on gem laboratories, see the chapter on diamond grading reports.

If you'd like more technical information on identifying man-made diamonds, consult the following sources:

"A Chart for the Separation of Natural and Synthetic Diamonds" by the Gemological Institute of America. It includes 60 color photographs.

Diamonds: Treatments, Synthetics and Simulants; Integrity, Disclosure and Detection, a CD-ROM produced by the Diamond Trading Company and distributed by GEM-A of the British Gemmological Association.

Guide to Laboratory-Created CVD & HPHT Diamonds: Methods of Growth, Techniques of Identification by Branko Deljanin, Sharrie Woodring, EGL, USA Group, 2004

The MicroWorld of Diamonds by John Koivula: Gemworld International, Northbrook, IL

Periodicals:

Australian Gemmologist. (Gemmological Association of Australia), Brisbane
Gems and Gemology. (Gemological Institute of America), Carlsbad, CA

Journal of Gemmology. (Gemmological Association and Gem Testing Laboratory of Great Britain), London

Diamond Types

In the 1930's, scientists divided diamonds into two basic categories— Type I and Type II. Type I diamonds can be broadly defined as diamonds with nitrogen in their structure; type II diamonds are those without significant nitrogen. This difference in structure affects the physical and optical properties of the diamonds. For example, Type II diamonds conduct heat better than Type I diamonds. They also absorb light differently and fluoresce in distinct ways.

If you decide to consult the preceding reference sources, it would be helpful for you to have a basic understanding of diamond types because researchers use these categories to classify lab-grown and HPHT-treated diamonds. If you only want to know how to evaluate natural diamonds, you can skip the rest of this section and go on to the next chapter.

Table 7.3: Features of Type Ia & Type Ib natural diamonds (those with nitrogen)

	Type Ia	Type Ib
Color	colorless to yellowish, yellow, brown, olive, gray; rare: green	fancy yellow, a more saturated yellow than Type Ia. All synthetic yellow diamonds with nitrogen fall in this category.
LW UV Fluorescence	none or typically weak to very strong blue	often none. Sometimes weak yellow or orange
SW UV Fluorescence	none or weak to strong blue.	often none. Sometimes weak yellow or orange,
Phosphorescence	occasionally weak yellow (LW & SW) , lasting 30 seconds or less.	occasionally weak to moderate yellow (LW & SW), usually less than 15 seconds
Electrical conductivity	none	none
Heat conductivity	very good	very good
Cleavage	relatively uneven	relatively uneven

Information in the above table is based on the *GIA Diamond Dictionary, Diamonds* by Eric Bruton, *Gemstone Enhancement* by Kurt Nassau, "A Chart for the Separation of Natural & Synthetic Diamonds" by GIA, *Gems & Gemology* and personal communication with Branko Deljanin., EGL USA Research.

Table 7.4: Features of Type IIa & Type IIb natural diamonds (without significant nitrogen)

	Type IIa (almost pure carbon with tiny amounts of nitrogen or boron)	**Type IIb** (boron substitutes for some carbon atoms)
Color	colorless, brown to light brown, and sometimes pink or blue-green	mostly blue, some gray
LW UV Fluorescence	none, weak blue, sometimes orange in pink diamonds	usually none, rarely weak to moderate orange to orange-red
SW UV Fluorescence	none or weak to medium blue or greenish gray sometimes orange in pink diamonds	usually none, occasionally weak to moderate yellow to bluish white, rarely orange to orange-red
Phosphorescence	usually none, Cullinan I, the largest faceted diamond in the world, phosphoreseces for several minutes	very rarely weak to moderate bluish-white to LW, almost always bluish-white to SW; rarely weak to moderate yellow, orange, or orange red to SW, less than 15 seconds.
Electrical conductivity	none	are semiconductors
Heat conductivity	3 to 5 times more heat conductive than Type I	varies from stone to stone
Cleavage	relatively perfect	relatively perfect

Information in the above table is based on the *GIA Diamond Dictionary*, *Diamonds* by Eric Bruton, *Gemstone Enhancement* by Kurt Nassau, "A Chart for the Separation of Natural & Synthetic Diamonds" by GIA, *Gems & Gemology*.and personal communication with Branko Deljanin, EGL USA and Alan Hodgkinson.

In the 1950's, it was proposed that Type II stones be further divided into Type IIa and Type IIb. Type II b diamonds phosphoresce and conduct electricity. Most natural blue diamonds are Type IIb.

Later Type I stones were divided into subtypes Ia and Ib. The nitrogen in Ib stones is distributed throughout the diamond crystal as single atoms and not concentrated in masses, while the nitrogen in Ia stones appears as pairs or clusters of atoms. Tables 7.3 and 7.4 summarize some of the characteristics of the four basic diamond types.

Most natural diamonds are Type Ia. Most HPHT synthetic diamonds are Type Ib, and most CVD diamonds are Type IIa. When diamonds fall in the same type category, it's harder to differentiate lab-created diamonds from those that are natural, and advanced spectrographic tests in gem labs are necessary.

The above four types can be further divided into additional sub-types, but that is beyond the scope of this chapter. For more information, consult the previously mentioned references.

8

Where's the Best Place to Buy a Diamond?

When people ask me where's the best place to buy a diamond, I usually tell them it depends on the type of diamond they want and the service they expect. Predicting where people can find the best stone and value for their money is not easy. I'd like to illustrate this with a true story about an aquamarine because the search for it involved a wide variety of merchants throughout the United States.

A friend of mine was about to celebrate her 30th birthday and wanted an aquamarine ring from her husband. After visiting several jewelry stores and finding nothing they liked, she asked me for help. My friend was looking for an aquamarine with the following characteristics.

◆ One to two carats in weight
◆ Light to medium light blue; shouldn't look colorless or resemble a sapphire or strong blue topaz
◆ Round, princess cut, fat oval, or squarish cushion shape
◆ Well-cut with no "window" when viewed straight down with the stone face-up (A window is a washed out area in the center of the stone that allows you to see right through it. Ideally the entire stone will reflect light and color back to the eye. Chapter 3 has photo examples.)

I first tried contacting some colored-gem dealers in Los Angeles. Even though they did have some well-cut large aquamarines, the ones in the 1- to 2-carat range had "windows." Then I called some gemstone cutters known for their high quality cuts, but they didn't have any aquamarines in the desired size range. During the next few months I looked for aquamarines whenever I took trips to various states to promote my books to the jewelry trade. Here's where I found some well-cut aquamarines in the correct color range:

◆ In an antique shop
◆ In a department store
◆ At two independent jewelers
◆ In a chain jewelry store at a mall.

The only aquamarine that met all of my friend's specifications was a princess cut in the mall store. However, the stone was mounted in a ring that my friend would not have liked, and the store wouldn't sell it loose.

Meanwhile I received a catalogue from an award-winning gem cutter with individual pictures of stones that he'd cut. Every stone shown looked well cut so I called him and asked if he had an aquamarine of the desired size. He had a 1.8-carat square radiant cut and the price was reasonable. After asking him to compare its color to that of other stones pictured in his catalogue, I did something I normally advise people not to do—I bought a colored gemstone from someone I didn't know without first looking at the stone. Why was I willing to do that? Here are some of the reasons:

◆ Because I was able to see several photo examples of his merchandise. None of the stones in his catalogue had a "window" so I knew that he could cut gemstones with good light refraction. In addition, most of his cuts were creative and unique.

◆ The cutter was able to answer all of my questions intelligently.

◆ I called him, he didn't call me; so I knew this wasn't a phone scam.

◆ He gave me the impression that he loved his work and wasn't only doing it for the money.

◆ I hadn't been able to find the right stone from anyone else. My first choice would have been to buy from someone I knew and trusted.

◆ The amount of money involved in the sale was not large.

◆ He had a 100% money back return policy. If you ever buy a gem without first looking at it, this is an essential condition.

◆ He accepted credit cards. It can be a lot easier to get money back from a credit card purchase than from one made with a check or debit card.

◆ I had an intuitive feel that I could trust him.

The stone had good light refraction but it was a little lighter in color and more greenish than I expected, but that's not surprising. Accurate color cannot be communicated with pictures on a printed page or on a computer monitor. One advantage of the aquamarine's color was that it looked natural rather than like the color of a treated blue topaz. My friend liked the aquamarine and had it custom set in a ring.

Finding a colorless or near colorless round diamond is a lot easier than finding an aquamarine. However, if you want a fancy color diamond or one with an unusual cut, it's possible that jewelers you know don't have it and can't get it for you. In that case you'll need to know how to select a jeweler. That's the topic of the rest of this chapter. But first I'll discuss a couple of the recommendations I gave in my first diamond book.

Why the *Diamond Ring Buying Guide* no longer has the Chapter "Is Your Jeweler a Crook?"

When my book the *Diamond Ring Buying Guide* was first published in 1989, it had a chapter on choosing a jeweler that was entitled "Is Your Jeweler a Crook?" Members of the press loved this title and so did many jewelry trade professionals. When I showed the book to salespeople in jewelry stores and they saw the chapter, they would often show it to their boss and jokingly say, "Look! This lady wrote about us in her book." A few other jewelers took offense.

One dealer read through my list of things to consider when choosing jewelers and asked me about the following questions I had included:

◆ What kind of credentials do they have?

◆ How long have they been in business?

◆ Are they members of professional trade organizations?

He mentioned the names of some long-time dealers and jewelers with high credentials who had ordered goods from suppliers just prior to declaring bankruptcy. In other words, they ordered merchandise without intending to pay for it. Then he asked me if paying dues to a trade organization really makes a jeweler more ethical or competent.

The more I thought about what he said, the more I realized that my chapter on choosing a jeweler was not as helpful to consumers as the information I gave them on diamond evaluation. So in 1996, when the book was completely revised and printed in color, I decided to replace the chapter "Is Your Jeweler a Crook?" with more diamond evaluation photos and information on diamond treatments.

Even though I've added a section on choosing a jeweler in this book, I still believe that the diamond information and photos I provide will be the most beneficial part of the book. You have to be knowledgeable about diamonds in order to determine if a salesperson is capable of helping you select an appropriate diamond. Additional information on selecting a jeweler can be found in the last chapter ("How to Avoid Ripoffs") in the section entitled "Three Stories of Satisfied Consumers."

Choosing a Jeweler

When buying diamonds, people are advised to consider the four C's of color, clarity, cut and carat weight. When selecting jewelers, I suggest that you consider the three C's of competence, candor and concern for the customer's welfare. Let's examine these three C's more closely.

Competence: How knowledgeable are the salespeople? Do they know how to evaluate gem and jewelry quality? Are they well informed about gem treatments?

One question you can ask to help determine their diamond competence is: **How would you describe the quality of the cut of this diamond(s)?** Salespeople should be able to compare diamonds with poor and mediocre cuts to those that are well cut and explain why any cut is inferior or superior. It's not sufficient for a salesperson to simply describe a diamond as a fine make or poor cut.

It's helpful for salespeople to give you proportion measurements, but this is not essential nor always possible. What's more important is that the salesperson understands the significance of any measurements that may be known about a diamond.

Any salesperson can read the clarity or color grade indicated on a diamond label or report. It requires skill, however, to provide information about cut quality just by looking at a diamond under magnification.

Competent salespeople are able to volunteer a variety of information about the diamonds and mountings in their store. If a salesperson can't do this, ask if there is somebody more knowledgeable who could assist you. The more informed salespeople are, the more capable they are of helping you make wise choices that fit your needs.

Candor: Do they tell you both the good and bad points of their inventory? Will they show you their diamonds under a microscope? Do they disclose gem treatments without your having to ask (colored gems are more likely to be treated than diamonds)? Do they explain quality and treatments in clear language, or do they just rely on trade euphemisms and marketing terms. The terminology jewelers use provides good clues about their ethics.

Concern for your Welfare: Do they listen to you and ask questions so they can determine what merchandise is best for you? Do they help you select mountings that will last and that are appropriate for your needs? Do they explain quality differences to you? Do they offer follow-up service? There are lots of jewelers who really care about their customers. It's to your advantage to establish a relationship with such a jeweler.

Using Product Knowledge & Intuition to Choose the Right Seller

Many people think that the best way for consumers to avoid ripoffs is to deal with sellers who have been in business for a long time and who are members of professional trade organizations. Even though this is often true, it isn't always the case. In addition, it's possible to spot qualified vendors without knowing their background. I'd like to illustrate this with an example unrelated to the gem trade. It involves the recent sale of my mother's house in a town a few hours from where I live.

A friend wanted to buy the house, but we needed comparable prices of others (called "comps") in the area. Since I was in charge of selling the property, I got some comps from four agents, one of whom I found by searching the Internet. I made an appointment with him even though the only facts I knew about him were his name (Ron), phone number and address, which was close to my mother's house.

When I arrived at Ron's office, he said, "Let's go have a look at the house." After we went through the place, he showed me all the research he'd done on the house. Even though I'd told him that we already had a buyer and planned to sell direct, he proceeded to tell me what needed to be done to sell the house and what he could do to make the process easier. He reviewed the sale prices of comparable homes and suggested a price range.

Ron was so forthcoming with his information and so skillful at selling me on the benefits of using his services, that the next day we signed a non-exclusive contract. Unfortunately the buyer we had lined up had to back for medical reasons, so Ron immediately began the process of selling the home.

Two days after he put up a for-sale sign, another buyer offered more than the asking price and ultimately purchased the house. Both buyers raved about what a wonderful agent Ron was. We all appreciated his informative, no-pressure approach to selling. We didn't need to know in advance that he had been in real estate for over 25 years; it was obvious that he was experienced by the way he answered our questions.

After I met Ron, I learned that he was a commercial real estate broker. Had I known this beforehand, I would have mistakenly assumed that he would either be disinterested or ineffectual in selling residential homes, and I would have never made an appointment with him.

Thanks to Ron, selling a house turned out to be a positive experience for me. However, I had done some advance research, so I knew what questions to ask, and I was able to tell immediately that Ron was a true professional.

Study this book carefully along with the *Diamond Ring Buying Guide*, visit a variety of jewelers, ask them questions and look at their diamonds under magnification. You may discover that you can learn more about jewelers by looking at their merchandise and talking to them than you can by reading their resumes.

Why this Book has No List of Recommended Jewelers

Several readers have asked me to list jewelers that I'd recommend along with their websites. Unfortunately, I don't have time to check them out and interview all their salespeople; furthermore, I'm not able to keep up with changes in their management, ownership, and staffing. Consequently, I've decided not to put recommendations in my book. I do, however, indicate the names of jewelers or dealers who provide photographs or information required for the book because it's professional courtesy to credit one's sources.

This book does have a list of major gem laboratories and their websites as well as the websites and addresses of appraisal and jewelry organizations. In addition, my website www.reneenewman.com lists independent jewelry appraisers who have passed gemological and appraisal exams. The chapter on appraisals gives you tips on interviewing them.

My goal is to keep my books and website as non-commercial as possible. This helps me to be more objective and open-minded than if I were trying to sell you diamonds or steer you to particular stores.

Looking for the Right Diamond

If this were an ideal world, it would be easy for consumers to find a competent, reliable jeweler offering attractive diamonds and mountings at affordable prices. In reality, it's hard to find everything you want at one store. If you do not have an established relationship with a jeweler and you have never looked at diamonds, you will probably have to visit several stores before you find an appropriate jeweler and before you know what kind of diamond you want and can afford.

I suggest that you visit a variety of types of stores from low end to high end and look at their diamonds with at least a loupe (Read Chapter One and ask the salespeople to show you how to use the loupe.) This will give you experience in looking at a range of diamond qualities without having to spend too much time with one salesperson. When you know what kind of diamond you want, you should spend more time examining diamonds under a microscope as well as with a loupe.

You may as well make the most of your time by also shopping for other jewelry items you might need. If you're looking for an engagement diamond you'll also want a ring as well as wedding bands for the bride and groom. Your visits to jewelry stores can also be an opportunity to shop for gifts for bridesmaids, birthdays and various holidays.

Keep an open mind and enter each store with positive expectations. At the very least you'll find what kind of diamond you *don't* want to buy and where you don't want to shop in the future. Meanwhile you are getting experience looking at diamonds, and you are learning how to spot competent and ethical salespeople as well as quality diamonds. You never know when or where the ideal gemstone will turn up; a number of people have told me they've found their diamonds and rings in unexpected places. (For example, the last chapter of this book tells about one couple who found their diamond in a combination rock shop/jewelry store, one which actually specialized in colored gemstones)

It's often more difficult to find a mounting you like than a diamond, and you may have to purchase them separately. There's a big advantage to having a diamond set at the store that sells you the diamond—it's reasonable to expect them to be fully responsible for any possible damage to the stone during setting, such as chipping.

When you compare diamond prices, keep in mind that you are not just paying for a gemstone; you're also paying for service, guarantees, and documentation. If you're buying a good quality diamond over one-half carat, it's advisable to purchase one accompanied by a lab report from a reputable lab. See the chapter on diamond grading reports for more information. Verify that the report matches the diamond by comparing the laser inscriptions (if present) and the placement of the inclusions. Jewelers also compare the measurements and the weights. Major diamond purchases should come with a 100% money-back return policy.

Sometimes consumers think they have to travel abroad or go to a big city with a diamond district in order to find a good diamond at a fair price, when in fact the right diamond may be in their home community. There are even historical examples of how people literally had diamonds, gold, silver and oil on their own land and never found them because they assumed these resources could only be found in distant places.

Some of these examples can be found in a short motivational book called *Acres of Diamonds* by Russel H. Conwell. It tells of a wealthy farmer named Ali Hafid who sold his farm in what is now India, and went to search for diamonds across the Middle East and into Europe. After he had spent all his money looking for diamonds and was in rags, he stood on the shore of a bay at Barcelona, Spain and cast himself into a tidal wave and drowned. Shortly thereafter, an unusual stone was found on Ali's farm.

It turned out to be a diamond. Further digging led to the discovery of the famous Golconda mine, which was right on Ali's property.

A more recent example from the book involved a Northern California rancher who had a passion for gold. When he heard that gold had been discovered in Southern California, he sold his ranch in 1847 so he could go search for gold there. The buyer of the ranch was Colonel Sutter, who discovered gold after he put a mill on a stream that ran through the ranch. The rancher could have become a millionaire if he had only looked for gold closer to home.

The moral of the stories and the book is that you don't have to search the world to find success, happiness and wealth because you have "Acres of Diamonds" where you now live. Ponder this, and start your search for a diamond right in your own home town.

9

Antique Cuts & Jewelry

The History of Diamond Cuts

It wasn't until the mid-1300's that European and Indian gem cutters began to cut and shape rough diamond. Compared to modern cuts, old cuts were very plain. The first was probably the **point cut**, which preserved the diamond crystal's octahedral shape and resembles two pyramids base to base. The sides were polished against a stationary polishing surface coated with diamond grit and olive oil.

The next to appear was the **table cut**, an octahedral shape with its top point cut away, creating a square-shaped, flat-top table facet. Frequently, cutters also removed the lower point of the stone to form a smaller square facet called a tabular. This gave the stone a total of ten facets—five on the crown (top) and five on the pavilion (bottom).

When such stone is viewed from above, the table cut looks like a square within a square. The table cut greatly improved the amount of light returned to the viewer, giving diamonds more brilliance and fire than point-cut gems. As a result, point-cut diamonds were gradually reshaped into table cuts. These dominated diamond jewelry through the 1500's.

Fig 9.1 Octahedron diamond crystal (shape of point cut). *Photo and diamond— Paul Cassarino.*

Fig 9.2 Table cut. *Photo by Paul Cassarino, diamond from the Gem Lab.*

Fig. 9.4 Rose-cut, pear-shape diamonds. *Photo of Victorian period earrings by Gail Levine.*

Left: Fig. 9.3 Briolette diamond earrings. *Earrings & photo from Harry Winston Inc.*

Rose Cut

The rose cut was probably developed in India in the early 1500's. **Rose-cut** diamonds are dome-shaped with flat bottoms and they have rose-petal-like triangular facets that radiate out from the center in multiples of six. From above, the rose cut may be round, oval or pear shape. Rose-cut diamonds can display considerable brilliance, but they don't have as much fire as a full-cut brilliant cut. The famous Orlov diamond is a form of rose cut.

During the 18th and 19th centuries, both Amsterdam and Antwerp specialized in rose cuts. The Dutch rose cut was more pointed than most others, while the Antwerp style was not as high or as steeply inclined. Most rose cuts were round. Oval and pear shapes were far more rare.

Variations of this cut are the **double rose** and the **briolette,** an elongated double rose that has a tear-drop shape. In recent years, rose cuts and briolettes have become very popular. In fact most rose cuts on the market are new, typically cut in India or Turkey. The demand for rose cuts started with designers, who use it for reproductions. The newer rose cuts tend to be more symmetrical while the shape and facets of most old rose-cut diamonds are normally irregular.

In the mid-1600's, the **single cut** was introduced. It had more potential for brilliance than the table cut because there were more facets: a table, eight crown facets, eight pavilion facets and sometimes a culet (the small facet on the pointed bottom of the pavilion). This cut served as the basis for the modern brilliant cut, and it is still used for small diamonds weighing less than one-tenth of a carat.

Fig. 9.5 Single cut. *Photo by Paul Cassarino.*

The **Mazarin cut** or **double cut** was also introduced in the 1600's. It consists of a cushion shape cut with seventeen facets above the girdle and seventeen below, including the culet. (A **cushion shape** has a rectangular or squarish outline with curved sides and rounded corners. It's an intermediary shape between a round and a square or an oval and a rectangle) The modern version of the double cut is the **Swiss cut**, a round 34-facet brilliant cut which is sometimes used for small stones.

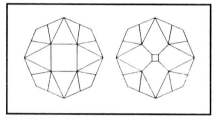 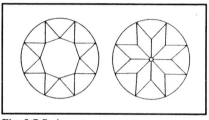

Fig. 9.6 Double cut (Mazarin cut)   **Fig. 9.7** Swiss cut

New developments in diamond cutting were aided by the industrial revolution and the discovery of diamonds in Brazil in the 1700's. Improved gas lighting, an increasing interest in optical science and a greater availability of diamonds encouraged diamond cutters to experiment with new faceting styles such as the **old-mine cut**—a cushion shape with a high crown, deep pavilion, large culet and 58 facets similar to the modern brilliant. "Old-miners" became the most popular cut diamonds of the eighteenth century.

Fig. 9.8 Old mine cut, face-up view   **Fig. 9.9** Side view of diamond in figure 9.8

Variations of the old-mine cut were the Brazilian and Lisbon cuts, which were fashioned from Brazilian diamonds. The generic name for these

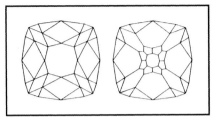

Fig. 9.10 Brazilian cut

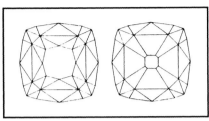

Fig. 9.11 Lisbon cut

cuts is brilliant-cut cushion or sim-ply **cushion**. This shape gradually went out of style for diamonds after the 1920's, but is becoming increasingly popular again.

Michael Goldstein, a specialist in old-cut diamonds, prefers the well-made cushions from around 1910 to many of those cut today. He says that a lot of people cutting cushions haven't looked at older ones. Consequently they're unable to cut cushions that look like an-tique diamonds.

Fig. 9.12 Modern cushion-cut diamond, flanked by two pear shapes (tw ≈20 carats). *Ring and photo from Harry Winston, Inc. See front cover for color photo of ring.*

The next cut to appear was the **old European cut**, which was similar to the old mine cut except it was round and sometimes less bulky. This new round cut is the direct ancestor of the modern brilliant cut. The old European cut is the most common diamond cut seen in antique jewelry. Don't expect to find true old-European cuts with high color grades. Their color grades tend to be lower than G color because the mines from which many of them originated, such as the Premier Mine in South Africa, did not produce much colorless rough.

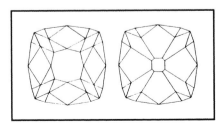

Fig. 9.13 Old-mine cut, a cushion shape

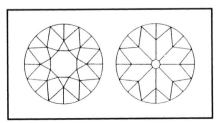

Fig. 9.14 Old European cut

Fig. 9.15 Old mine cut, 1.13 ct

Fig. 9.16 Recut to 0.78-ct radiant cut

Fig. 9.17 Old mine cut, 0.64-ct

Fig. 9.18 Recut to 0.41-ct radiant cut

Fig. 9.19 Old mine cut, 1.71 ct

Fig. 9.20 Recut to 1.39 round brilliant cut

Figs. 9.15–9.20 Compare the diamonds above. As diamond cutting has progressed, the culets have become smaller and the shapes more symmetrical. The diamonds in these photos were recut for customers of Joe & Paul Cassarino at the Gem Lab in Rochester, New York. *All photos by Paul R. Cassarino.*

Fig. 9.21 Old European cut, 1.24 ct with a diameter of 6.72 mm before being recut. *Photo by Paul R. Cassarino.*

Fig. 9.22 Same diamond recut to 1.03 ct, 6.50 mm, round brilliant ideal cut. *Photo by Paul R. Cassarino.*

Old mine and old European cuts are sometimes recut as modern cuts in order to make them brighter and more symmetrical (figs 9.16–9.22). They may also just be repolished. However, occasionally modern cuts are recut as old European cuts.

According to Debra Sawatzky, an antique jewelry specialist, there's been an unusually high demand lately for Old European cuts. It's sometimes easiest to meet this demand by recutting round brilliants. So don't assume that rings mounted with old European cuts are antiques. Even if the diamonds are truly old, this doesn't mean the ring is old. It's not uncommon to remount old stones in new jewelry.

A Boston diamond cutter, Henry Morse, is credited with proposing the proportions and angles for the modern round brilliant cut in the late 1800's, but the old-European and old-mine cuts remained popular into the 20th century. The **modern round brilliant cut** has a lower crown, a smaller culet and more brilliance than its predecessors, but it has the same number of facets—33 on the crown and 25 on the pavilion, including the culet. Since about 1920, it's been the best-selling diamond cut. The diamond cutter, Marcel Tolkowksy, helped popularize the modern round brilliant by publishing his recommendations for its best proportions in 1919 in a treatise called *Diamond Design*.

The girdles of high-quality diamonds are usually faceted to help reflect light internally and to give the diamond a more finished look. This means

Fig. 9.23 Old Asscher cut. *Photo by Gail Levine from the Auction Market Resource.*

Fig. 9.24 Royal Asscher® Cut. *Photo from the Royal Asscher Diamond Co.*

that most round brilliants have more than 58 facets. The brilliant cut is also applied to shapes other than round such as the marquise, pear, oval and heart shapes.

Another cut that appeared in the late 1800's was the square or rectangular **emerald cut**, which had step-like, four-sided facets that are parallel to the girdle, unlike the brilliant cut which has triangular facets and kite-shaped facets. In addition, the corners of the stone were cut off creating eight sides and a more rounded look. Joseph Asscher is credited with developing this style. Consequently old square or rectangular emerald cuts are often called **Asscher cuts** or simply Asschers.

Unlike modern emerald cuts, old Asschers had smaller tables, higher crowns and deeper pavilions. Despite their greater depth, they are noted for their high brilliance and dispersion. Nevertheless, many were recut into flatter emerald or radiant cuts to create a more contemporary look. Today old Asscher cuts are in high demand and are selling at a premium, so it would be pointless to recut them.

In 2001, the Royal Asscher Diamond Company introduced a new patented square emerald cut to the market called the Royal Asscher® Cut. It's an offspring of the original Asscher diamonds, but it has 16 additional facets giving it a total of 74 facets.

The Royal Asscher Company did two years of research and computer simulations to determine which combinations of angles and proportions would maximize the brilliance of a square emerald cut. Besides optimizing the life of the stone, the new Royal Asscher utilizes the rough more efficiently. As a result, it looks larger for its weight face up because the total depth is less. Royal Asscher diamonds are cut and polished exclusively in Amsterdam, Holland and are inscribed with the Royal Asscher Cut logo and an identification number held by the company.

Unlike the Royal Asscher, the old Asschers are not perfect squares. Some look more rectangular than square. In addition, old Asschers had smaller tables, higher crowns and no girdle inscriptions. So it's not hard to distinguish between the two Asschers. No matter which Asscher you might own, they are both beautiful diamond cuts.

Some diamonds that were cut in the 1930's and 1940's are called **transitional cuts**. Dealer Michael Goldstein says these stones usually have the overall faceting of modern brilliants but still may have a slightly open culet and a bit of the faceting of an old European cut. According to Goldstein, the term "transitional cut" can also refer to a stone that is a cross between a cushion cut and an old European cut or it may mean a stone that is out of round with attributes of the cushion cut. A transition is the process of changing from one state (cutting style) to another, hence the term "transitional."

In the late 1970's Henry Grossbard of New York patented a rectangular brilliant cut diamond with slanted corners. He called it the **radiant** cut, (figs 9.16 and 9.18). It was the first rectangular cut to have brilliant-cut facets on both the crown and the pavilion.

The **princess cut** appeared around 1980. It was a square brilliant cut that retained its 90-degree-angle corners. In other words, it had a true square shape. The Quadrillion® is a precision-cut square brilliant that was patented in 1981. It has 49 facets and a star-shaped pattern on the pavilion.

Some diamond crystals are flattened and triangular in shape with two individuals sharing a common face. These twinned crystals are called **macles** and are typically fashioned into heart, pear and triangle shapes to make efficient use of the rough. Originally the triangles were given a tabular or step cut, but in the 1950's, cutters began to experiment with new faceting patterns to increase their brilliance.

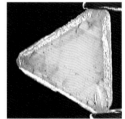

Fig. 9.25 Macle. *Photo by Paul Cassarino.*

The Royal Asscher Diamond Company produced a brilliant-cut triangle with arching sides in 1960 and named it the **trilliant**. In 1962, Irving and Milton Meyer created an American version with straight sides called the American trilliant. Then in 1978 Leon and Marvin Finker trademarked their version of a triangular brilliant-cut the **trillion**. It had equilateral sides and straight edges. They re-registered their cut as the **Trielle®** because "trillion" had passed into common use as a name for any triangular brilliant cut.

Knowing when the various diamond cuts first entered the market can help you determine the age of a jewelry piece. For example, if someone shows you an antique-style ring with a princess-cut diamond, it's probably safe to bet that it wasn't made before 1980.

Pricing Antique Diamonds

The main types of antique diamonds found on the market today are old European cuts , old mine cuts, briolettes and rose cuts. Old Asscher cuts are hard to find and most come with old mountings, which helps differentiate them from the modern Asscher-cut diamonds. Because of their rarity, old Asscher cuts normally cost more than modern emerald cuts.

Antique diamonds are priced using the same color, clarity and weight criteria as modern cuts. However, there are some fundamental differences:

◆ Old cuts are worth more mounted in their original mounting than when they are loose. With antique jewelry, the sum of the whole is worth more than the sum of the parts.

◆ Old cuts are subject to wider variations in pricing than modern cuts. This is partly because there's a more limited supply of antique diamonds and partly because they have enormous differences in symmetry since they were not cut with modern machinery.

◆ The proportions of antique diamonds are not as important as they are for new diamonds. Usually the older the diamonds, the poorer the cut by today's standards because weight retention of the rough was once more important than brilliance. Nevertheless cut does matter. Large, poorly cut diamonds may be worth as much as 50% less than well-proportioned stones of similar color and clarity.

The way a stone is cut can indicate whether it is an antique diamond or a newly cut antique-style diamond. Newly cut diamonds often have thicker girdles, lower crowns and different faceting patterns than their earlier counterparts; thus reflecting the light differently. Conversely, knife-edge girdles are common on old cushion cuts.

Appraisers determine the value of antique diamonds by a variety of methods. Sometimes they base the value on the hammer prices of similar diamonds at auctions. The best and most convenient source of diamond prices at auctions is the *Auction Market Resource* by Gail Levine. Sales of selected pieces from all the major auction houses are listed together with detailed descriptions and sales prices. For more information consult www.auctionmarketresource.com.

Appraisers often consult the prices listed on antique diamond websites such as www.antiquediamond.com or they may call antique dealers or jewelers for price information. Price lists of new diamonds are also used as a reference tool. No matter which method is used, the value will vary depending on the purpose of the appraisal—estate, insurance replacement, orderly liquidation (through auctions) or quick liquidation.

The quick liquidation value is the immediate cash amount that you can get for a diamond or jewelry piece if you try to sell it. The least expensive way to determine this value is to show the piece to some antique dealers or jewelers that sell estate jewelry and ask them how much they'd pay for it. If you're looking for the highest possible price, don't take the jewelry to a general pawn shop. Most likely the pawn shop will only give you a low scrap price; they're not normally trained to know the antique value of jewelry unless they happen to sell a lot of estate jewelry.

No matter what type of appraisal you get, expect differences of opinion among appraisers and sellers. There is no one true value for an antique diamond or any other diamond, for that matter. For information on selecting an appraiser, consult the appraisal chapter in this book.

Period Jewelry (European & American)

Antique dealers often describe their styles of jewelry with a period name based on the rule of monarchs or art movements. Many of the periods overlap, and the beginning and starting dates vary depending on the historical source. The dates and information in this section are based largely on Christie Romero's *Warman's Jewelry*, Gail Levine's *Auction Market Resource*, and Anna Miller's *Buyer's Guide to Affordable Antique Jewelry*.

Before listing the various jewelry periods, let's define some related terminology:

Antique jewelry: Any jewelry one-hundred or more years old, as defined by the United States Customs Bureau. Webster's dictionary defines the term "antique" more loosely—any work of art or the like from an early period.

Heirloom, estate, or vintage jewelry: Jewelry that has been previously owned by someone and that is typically passed on from one generation to another. It can range from a few decades to 100 or more years in age.

Collectibles: Items gathered from a specific designer, manufacturer, or any period or periods in time. The items are collected according to the buyer's interests, and normally they are no longer in production, but they don't have to be as old as antiques. For example, retro jewelry pieces are considered collectibles, but they are not true antiques. Hence the phrase, "antiques and collectibles."

Circa dating: Establishing an approximate date of origin for a jewelry piece. It covers a ten-year window on either side of the date. A circa date of 1900 means the piece was probably made some time between 1890 and 1910.

Jewelry Periods

Here's an outline of jewelry eras starting from the 18th Century followed by brief descriptions of each period.

Georgian   1714–1837 (reigns of King George I – King George IV)
Early Victorian 1837–1860 (Queen Victoria 1837–1901)
Mid-Victorian: 1860–1885
Late Victorian: 1885–1901
Arts & Crafts: 1890–1914
Art Nouveau: 1890–1910
Edwardian: 1890–1915 (King Edward VII, 1901–1910) (Belle Epoque)
Art Deco: 1915–1935
Retro: 1935–1955

Georgian (1714–1837)

Most of the diamond jewelry during the Georgian period was hand-fabricated with 18K or 22K gold. In the early 1800's in England, gold filigree was popular. Diamonds were commonly set in silver over gold to bring out their whiteness. Diamond brilliance was intensified by foil backing the stones in closed-back mountings. The backs began to open up in the late Georgian period after 1780.

The discovery of diamonds in Brazil during this period along with the advancement of cutting techniques led to variations of the 58-facet, cushion- shaped old mine brilliant cut. Two variations were the Brazilian cut and the Lisbon cut.

In 1750, an English jeweler named David Jeffries wrote that the brilliant cut was a whim of fashion and that the rose cut would outlive it. He was wrong. Over the next two centuries many of the old roses were recut to brilliant form with a major loss of weight. Nevertheless, rose-cut diamonds can also be found in jewelry of this period.

Fig. 9.26 Georgian brooch with rose-cut diamonds. *Photo by Gail Levine*

Fig. 9.27 Georgian brooch with rose-cut diamonds. *Photo by Gail Levine.*

Fig. 9.28 Georgian brooch with rose-cut diamonds. *Photo by Gail Levine*

Fig. 9.29 Georgian ring. *Photo by Gail Levine.*

The themes of the jewelry designs were often from nature—flowers, leaves, acorns, birds and feathers. The designs began to combine colored gemstones such as aquamarine, garnets and pink topaz with the Brazilian diamonds.

Both women and men wore a lot of jewelry during the Georgian era. Men even wore jeweled buttons on their coats and jeweled buckles on their shoes. Women had full or partial ensembles of jewelry with matching necklaces, earrings, brooches, rings and bracelets. The full ensembles were called **parures** and the partial ensembles, **demiparures**. One unusual type of jewelry piece was the aigrette, a hair or hat brooch ornament. Some aigrettes trembled when the wearer moved.

Don't expect to find jewelry from the Georgian period at your local antique store. It's very rare.

Victorian (1837–1901)

Queen Victoria was a diamond lover, and she was the trend-setter for the wealthy people of Britain's new industrial society. In the early Victorian period, most diamonds were rose cuts or old mine cuts, but by the end of the 19th century, they were outnumbered by the old European cut, which some people called the Victorian cut.

In the mid and late Victorian periods, diamonds were plentiful, especially after the discovery of diamonds in South Africa in 1867 and the introduction of electric lighting in the 1880's, which helped diamonds sparkle indoors and at night. Closed and foiled settings were gradually replaced with open-back mountings, and there was a greater variety of setting styles—bezel, prong, gypsy and wirework settings. In 1886, Tiffany & Co. introduced a high-prong setting for diamond solitaires that became the standard for engagement rings; it was appropriately called the "Tiffany setting."

Gold was also readily available during the Victorian period, thanks to discoveries in California (1848), Australia (1851) Black Hills, South Dakota (1874), South Africa (1886), Yukon, Canada (1895), and Alaska (1898). Most of the early Victorian diamond jewelry was hand-crafted using 18K to 22K gold, some of it tricolor. But in 1854, the British government made 9K, 12K, and 15K gold legal in order to meet foreign competition. Jewelers in Britain were not required to mark their jewelry during most of the nineteenth century, so it's not uncommon for jewelry during this period to be unmarked.

By the end of the Victorian era, a high percentage of the gold jewelry was machine-made and mass produced. Platinum jewelry had also been introduced to the market, but it was generally made by hand.

Victorian jewelry displayed a wide variety of motifs—branches, shells, knots, buckles, plants, flowers, vines, insects, clasped hands and women with flowing hair. After the death of Queen Victoria's husband Prince Albert (1861), mourning jewelry with black onyx or jet became popular.

Many of the World's most famous jewelry firms were founded during the Victorian period; for example, Tiffany's in 1837, Cartier in 1847, and Boucheron in 1858.

Fig. 9.30 Portrait brooch accented by diamonds and pearls. *Brooch from D & E Singer; photo by Robert Weldon.*

Fig. 9.31 Victorian brooch, rose-cuts

Fig. 9.32 Victorian bracelet, old European cut

Fig. 9.33 Victorian brooch

Fig. 9.34 Victorian ring

Fig. 9.35 Victorian ring

Fig. 9.36 Victorian brooch set with old European cut diamonds

Fig. 9.37 Victorian brooch

Figs. 9.31–9.37 Photos of Victorian jewelry from Gail Levine. These pictures can be viewed in color on www.auctionmarketresource.com along with over 12,000 other photographs of antique jewelry and collectibles.

Arts & Crafts Movement (1890–1910)

The Arts & Crafts movement coincided with three other schools of design—traditional Edwardian, Art Nouveau (New Art) and Late Victorian. It was a reaction to the mass-produced jewelry of the industrial revolution and the lavish ornamentation of the Victorian era.

Arts & Crafts jewelry was entirely hand-made and the materials were inexpensive. Instead of gold and platinum, silver, brass and copper were the preferred metals. Cabochon turquoise, agate, amber, moonstones and opals replaced diamonds, rubies and emeralds and were usually bezel set. The designs were either abstract or featured themes of nature such as flowers, leaves and birds.

Art Nouveau (1890–1910)

The "New Art" period is known for its flowing curved lines, botanical motifs and bright colors. It was the beginning of modern jewelry design. Many French jewelers adopted this style, but the one best known for his designs and artistry was René Lalique. He combined expensive gems with inexpensive materials like ivory and horn and set them in 18K gold. One of the techniques Lalique is noted for and that became associated with Art Nouveau is *plique à jour* enameling—translucent enamel with no metal backing, which resembles a stained glass window.

In contrast to earlier periods, diamonds, rubies, emeralds and sapphires were used mainly as accents for larger cabochon-cut semi-precious stones such as lapis lazuli, moonstone, malachite, carnelian, marcasite and conch pearls. Synthetic rubies and emerald triplets (two pieces of colorless beryl joined with a layer of green cement) made their appearance in Art Nouveau jewelry. The motifs most frequently seen are women with flowing hair, human forms with insect wings, butterflies, peacocks, bees, swans, snakes and flowers. Silver, gold, copper and plated metals were all used in this jewelry.

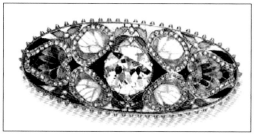

Fig. 9.38 Art nouveau brooch with old European cut diamond. *Photo by Gail Levine.*

Fig. 9.39 Art nouveau brooch. *Photo by Gail Levine.*

Edwardian (also known as **Belle Epoque**) (1890–1915)

The heavy use of diamonds, platinum and pearls in delicate, lacelike mountings are chief characteristics of this jewelry. Even though the reign of Edward VII was only from 1901–1910, the lavish court style of the era influenced fashion in the decades before and after his rise to power.

Edwardian jewelry was also inspired by the French courts of Louis XV and Louis XVI. In fact, it was the French jeweler Louis Cartier (1875–1942) who was in the forefront of developing this style and who was an official jeweler for the English court. As a result, it's also identified as *belle epoque*, the French term for "beautiful era." Another expression that is sometimes used is the "garland style" (*style garlande* in French) because garlands (wreaths) of flowers and leaves were typical motifs for this jewelry. Other motifs included horseshoes, doves, fish, ducks, hearts, sun, stars, moon and bows and arrows.

New cuts such as the marquise, the emerald cut and the baguette emerged during this period, thanks to improvements in diamond-cutting technology. Calibrated stones of standardized sizes and shapes became available for use in mass produced jewelry. Cushion cuts, old European cuts and rose cuts remained popular; and briolette diamonds were often suspended in earrings.

After the development of a torch hot enough to work platinum (about 1890), platinum became the most common metal for fine pieces. For awhile, platinum was laminated to gold much like silver had been. But gradually it became evident that platinum was strong enough to be used

Fig. 9.41 Edwardian platinum, diamond bar pin. *Brooch and photo from Joseph DuMouchelle Intl. Auctioneers; David Frechette Photography.*

by itself for intricate mountings and secure diamond settings. Millegrained (raised beaded edges) platinum settings were used to make diamonds look larger and knife-edge settings were created to make the mounting appear invisible. Much of the metalwork was open, allowing fabric to show through. During World War I, white gold came into common use because platinum was temporarily banned for use in jewelry

Even though Edwardian jewelry was mostly white, pastel colors were also in fashion and later it was set with darker colored gemstones such as amethyst, alexandrite, amethyst, chrysoprase and demantoid garnets.

Fig 9.42 Edwardian lavalier

Fig. 9.43 Edwardian diamond brooch

Fig. 9.44 Edwardian rose-cut barrette

Fig. 9.45 Edwardian pendant

Fig. 9.46 Pin-pendant

Fig. 9.47 Old European cut diamond ring

Fig. 9.45 Edwardian pendant

Figs. 9.42–9.45 Photos of Edwardian diamond jewelry from Gail Levine. These pictures can be viewed in color on www.auctionmarketresource.com along with over 12,000 other photographs of antique jewelry and collectibles.

Some of the noted French houses who created Edwardian jewelry were Boucheron, Cartier, Chaumet, Georges Fouquet and LaCloche Frères. In the United States, it was made by Tiffany & Co., Black Starr & Frost, Marcus & Company, etc. Most of the pieces of the Russian Imperial court jeweler Peter Carl Fabergé (1846–1920) can be classified as Edwardian, but others have Art Nouveau lines and motifs.

Art Deco (1915–1935)

Geometric patterns, straight lines and bold color contrasts characterize Art Deco designs. Platinum, diamonds and white gold continued to be used extensively, but there was a greater use of colored gemstones, some of which were synthetic. Lapis, jade, coral and black onyx were especially popular.

Even though old European, single and rose cuts were still present, the modern brilliant cut in round and fancy shapes was more commonplace. New shapes for side stones emerged in the form of bullets, half moons and shields.

One of the most popular articles of jewelry was the diamond straightline bracelet, which in the 1980's was revived and called the tennis bracelet. The cocktail wristwatch, pendant watch and dress clip were other innovations of the Art Deco period.

The motifs most often found were geometric, abstract, floral, Oriental and Egyptian. The latter two followed the discovery of King Tutankhamun's tomb in 1923 and new trade agreements between Japan and the US.

Louis Cartier is the most famous Art Deco designer. The works of Van Cleef and Arpels also had a strong influence on the period. Other leading designers and houses were Mauboussin, Jean Fouquet, Boucheron, Chaumet, LaLoche and the American firms of Tiffany & Co, Black, Starr & Frost, J.E. Caldwell & Co., C.D. Peacock, Harry Winston, and Shreve, Crump & Low.

Retro (1935–1955)

The all-white look of diamonds and platinum began to fade during the Great Depression of the early 1930's. Then when platinum was declared a strategic metal by the US government during World War II, it was no longer used as a jewelry metal in America. It was replaced in fine jewelry by yellow gold and rose gold, and later by white gold.

Colored gems such as citrine, aquamarine and tourmaline were typically used instead of diamonds, although diamond pavé did continue to enhance designs. Masses of baguettes were used in channel-set jewelry.

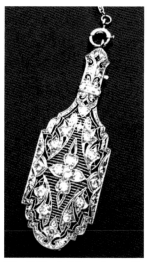

Fig. 9.46 Art Deco lorgnette

Fig. 9.47 Watch

Fig. 9.48 Art Deco brooch

Fig. 9.49 Art Deco brooch

Fig. 9.50 Ring

Fig. 9.52 Lapel watch

Fig. 9.53 Art Deco watch

Fig. 9.51 Art Deco clips

Fig. 9.54 Art Deco brooch

Figs. 9.46–9.54 Photos of Art Deco diamond jewelry from Gail Levine. These pictures can be viewed in color on www.auctionmarketresource.com along with over 12,000 other photographs of antique jewelry and collectibles.

Fig. 9.55 Retro brooch

Fig. 9.56 Retro ring

Fig. 9.58 Watch

Fig. 9.59 Watch $ clip

Fig. 9.57 Retro watch ring

Fig. 9.61 Watch

Fig. 9.60 Retro ring

Fig. 9.62 Retro ring

Figs. 9.55–9.62 Photos of Retro period diamond jewelry from Gail Levine. These pictures can be viewed in color on www.auctionmarketresource.com along with over 12,000 other photographs of antique jewelry and collectibles.

Hollywood stars influenced fashion more than royalty, and France was no longer the jewelry design center of the world. The designs were bold, bracelets had heavy links, pendants were large and were made so they could convert to brooches.

In 1948, DeBeer's launched their famous slogan "a diamond is forever." Platinum returned after the war and was used to create lighter weight jewelry and wire settings that held clusters of diamonds, many of which had pear, oval and marquise shapes. By the end of the Retro period, diamonds were once again a girl's best friend.

10

Recutting Diamonds

Even though diamonds are the hardest substance on earth, they can break and chip. Fortunately, though, if they are damaged, recutting can usually make them look like new. Other reasons why diamonds are recut:

◆ To make them look more modern

◆ To make them look antique

◆ To improve their brilliance

◆ To improve their cut grade

◆ To improve their color grade

◆ To intensify the color of fancy color diamonds

◆ To improve their clarity

Perhaps you're wondering why diamonds aren't always initially cut to maximize their brilliance and produce the best possible color and clarity. Usually it's because the cutter wanted to retain as much weight as possible from the original diamond crystal in order to maximize its value. As the weight of a diamond goes down, its value can decrease in two ways:

a. **Its per-carat price can go down.** When a diamond moves down from one weight category to another, its price per carat may go down. There's an especially large decrease in price when a diamond falls below a true half carat or full carat. That's because one-carat diamonds are in high demand and they are more rare. Diamonds with the highest color and clarity grades have the highest price differentials as they move up or down from one weight category to another.

b. **Its total price will go down.** For example, a 0.95-carat diamond that sells for $7000 per carat would cost $6650 (0.95 x $7000), which is $350 less than a one carater of the same per-carat price.

When diamonds are cut with excellent proportions, they usually weigh less than if they were poorly cut. In order to make up the difference in price, sellers have to charge more for well-cut diamonds than for those that are cut mainly for weight retention.

Diamond cutting is an art and skill that involves making a compromise between two factors—maximum beauty and maximum value. However in most instances, the potential value and salability of the finished diamond is what determines how a diamond is initially cut and whether a diamond is worth recutting.

Fig. 10.1 A rough culet in a VS₁ diamond

The diamond in figure 10.1 is an example of how cutters maximize value. This VS₁ diamond has a rough culet and weighs 0.995 carats (1.00 carat when rounded to two decimal points). Polishing away the roughness might have brought the weight down to 0.99 carats, but it would not have increased the clarity grade. Consequently, the culet was left unpolished. The rough culet is not visible to the naked eye, nor does it decrease the brilliance of the diamond. Buyers who depend only on grades and who don't examine diamonds under magnification would never notice it. If the roughness prevented a sale, the stone could be easily repolished, but with a possible loss of weight.

Because of technological advances, the concept of diamond beauty has evolved over the years. Five hundred years ago, it wasn't possible to cut a round brilliant diamond. At that time, viewing poorly polished, unsymmetrical rose-cut diamonds was probably a breath-taking experience because they were so unusual and they sparkled more than existing table cuts. Times have changed.

The previous chapter showed examples of two old mine cuts that were recut as radiants and one that was recut as a round. When the diamonds were first fashioned, they may have been considered exquisite, but after the new owners compared their brilliance to contemporary cuts, they decided recutting was worthwhile, even though their stones would become smaller.

Fig. 10.2a Old mine cut, 2.40 ct, M/SI$_2$, before it was recut as a round brilliant

Fig. 10.2b Recut to 1.80-carat, L/VVS$_2$, ideal cut

Fig. 10.3a Old European cut, 1.24 carats

Fig. 10.3b Recut to 1.03-carat ideal cut

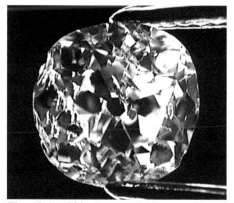

Fig. 10.4a Old mine cut, 0.77 carats, JI$_1$, AGS cut 10

Fig. 10.4b Recut to 0.57 carat, I/I$_1$, ideal AGS cut 0

All photos on this page were taken by Paul R. Cassarino of The Gem Lab.

There are times, however, when people choose to retain the old cutting style because it can enhance the value of antique jewelry. Sometimes estate dealers send old European and old mine cut stones to cutters just for a spruce-up job. The abrasions and bruises may just be polished away and the size of the culet may be reduced.

As I mentioned in the previous chapter, many diamonds are being fashioned with antique-style cuts. Nevertheless they are being cut with better symmetry and a higher polish than was possible two hundred years ago, which is one way of distinguishing newly cut diamonds from authentic old ones.

Figures 10.2a–10.4b show how both the brilliance and value of diamonds can increase with recutting. These stones were recut for clients of Joe and Paul Cassarino, jeweler-gemologists at The Gem Lab in Rochester, New York. Not only was there a major improvement in the cut grade of the first diamond in figure 10.2a, but its clarity went up five grades from an SI_2 to a VVS_2, and its color went up one grade from an M to an L.

A chip was removed from the old European cut in figure 10.3a, and it was also recut to American ideal proportions, while remaining above one carat in weight.

The color also went up one grade for the diamond in figure 10.4a, and it can now be sold at a premium because it has an AGS ideal cut grade of 0. This stone, by the way, is an example of how a diamond with an imperfect clarity grade can still be very desirable.

How do Cutters Modify Diamond Color?

Yellowish tints of color can be removed from diamonds by subjecting them to high-temperatures and high pressure. That is considered an unnatural color change. The color grade can also be improved without subjecting the diamond to any unnatural processes. A cutter can sometimes raise the color grade of a diamond by:

a. **The removal of excess weight**. The heavy pavilions of old mine cuts often intensify the color. That is why the color grade of diamonds 10.2a and 10.4a went up when their pavilions were cut to modern standards.

   In the case of fancy color diamonds, cutters want to intensify the color. That's why it's not uncommon for fancy color diamonds to have excess weight. Maximum color is more important than maximum brilliance.

b. **The choice of shape and faceting style**. For example, a fancy light yellow round brilliant can sometimes be recut into a fancy intense yellow radiant. However there may be a weight loss of 20–25%.

Because of this, yellow rough is more often than not cut as radiants or princess cuts. The color is intensified and more weight is retained. Rounds typically undergo a greater weight loss and can look lighter. Consequently fancy intense yellow round brilliants typically sell at premiums of 15–100% over radiants of the same size, color and clarity grade.

You may wonder how cut can change the color of a diamond. It doesn't actually change it; it just makes the color appear different face up. The round and radiant in the above example had the same color when viewed from the side. Unlike colorless diamonds, fancy color diamonds are graded face-up instead of from the side. The way the facets are designed to reflect light back to the eye can change the apparent color of a diamond, giving the diamond a different color grade.

c.. **The way the girdle is cut**. If the bruted (unpolished) girdle of diamonds with G–D color grades are faceted, their color can improve by one grade. Curiously, the opposite effect can occur with stones below H color. For example, if you facet the girdle of a low J color diamond, it can become a K color. (Source: Barry Rogoff, a diamond cutter in Los Angeles).

d. **The position of color zoning within the stone**. Sometimes diamonds have bands or sections of color called **zoning**. If a cutter orients the stone so the color falls in an area such as the culet, the color may reflect throughout the stone.

One unusual example, according to Rogoff, involves a 22-carat octahedral rough diamond that was vivid pink. The owner wanted to make a matching pair of rounds. When the cutter sawed the crystal in half, one part remained pink and the other was D color. The color zoning of the rough had not been visible prior to cutting. Unfortunately, there was a major reduction in value because vivid pink diamonds are extremely rare and sell for a lot more than D color diamonds.

Getting your Diamond(s) Recut

You may have diamonds that you think are beyond repair. It is amazing how a badly damaged stone can be transformed into a beautiful one. (See examples 10.5a–10.7b). Or you may have dull-looking diamonds that you wish had more life. If so, consider showing them to a reputable jeweler.

There is always a risk of breakage when recutting diamonds. In addition, it takes a lot of skill to bring out their maximum beauty. Consequently, it's to your advantage to have your diamonds assessed by experienced jewelers

Fig. 10.5a Damaged 0.86-ct round brilliant

Fig. 10.5b Same diamond recut to 0.70 ct

Fig. 10.6a Chipped 1.01-ct old European cut

Fig. 10.6b Recut to 0.78 round brilliant

Fig. 10.7a Damaged 1.15 ct round brilliant

Fig. 10.7b Same diamond recut to 0.86 ct

All photos on this page were taken by Paul R. Cassarino of The Gem Lab

who consider the quality of cut a priority and who can explain it to you clearly. They are more likely to have contacts with highly skilled cutters than sellers who feature bargain diamonds.

After you find a jeweler who can offer recutting services, ask to see an example of what the diamond will look like when recut. Then place the stone next to your diamond. If you see a dramatic difference in appearance, recutting could be worthwhile. Find out how much weight could be lost and ask about the risk of breakage. The jeweler may have to send the stone to the cutter to get this information.

Good cutters will look for inclusions in the diamond that might threaten its durability, and they will probably check it with a viewing instrument called a polariscope to determine if there is stress. If the stone displays vibrant colors between the crossed polarized lenses of the polariscope, this indicates strain in the diamond. If a diamond is not a good candidate for recutting, the cutter will probably advise against it, but this is rarely necessary. Most diamonds can be safely recut. The cutter will also estimate the weight loss and then the jeweler will relay that information to you.

The cost of cutting varies depending on the weight of the diamond and the amount of work required. Typical charges for recutting are $300–$400 per carat. Simple polishing and minor repairs will cost less. If the diamond breaks, it's considered an "act of God" and no liability is assumed. When dealing with skilled cutters, breakage is typically not a problem.

The cutter may propose different options. For example, if you had a chipped 3.06-carat stone, he might propose keeping the stone at 3 carats by smoothing away the chip and leaving the stone out of round. The cutter may also propose recutting the entire stone to excellent proportions despite the fact that the stone may end up weighing just 2.25 carats. There are often a variety of options—simple repolishing, minor repairs, no action, or complete recutting. In the end, your goals and your wallet will determine the best course of action.

11

Diamond Grading Reports

The first diamond grading reports were issued by the GIA (Gemological Institute of America) Gem Trade Laboratory in 1955. The GIA intentionally chose not to call them "certificates" because doing so would appear to validate the diamond itself, rather than objectively reporting information about the stone. Some other labs use the term "certificate" and trade members often refer to grading reports as "certs." No labs, however, guarantee that their grades are accurate. In other words, diamond grades are never legally certified.

The color and clarity grades of the GIA grading report are based on a system developed by the GIA in 1952. Prior to that time, diamond color was described inconsistently in the trade with terms such as "River" and "Top Wesselton" or with multiple grades such as "A," "AA," and "AAA."

Since the GIA was the first to develop a diamond grading system and report, their reports are the best known in the industry and enjoy a worldwide reputation. Another internationally respected diamond report is the one issued in Antwerp Belgium by the HRD (abbreviation of the Flemish name Hoge Raad voor Diamant). First introduced in 1976, the HRD Diamond Certificate is better known in Europe, Africa and Asia than in North America. The volume of diamonds graded at the HRD and GIA is so high that it can sometimes take weeks to receive a grading report. This is one reason why other labs have emerged.

Two other laboratories that issue a high volume of diamond grading reports are IGI (International Gemological Institute) and the EGL USA Group, and there also several more. Some labs are known for being more strict than others in their grading. Since reputations can vary from one lab and location to another, it's best to do some research on the labs in your area. Ask a few jewelers and maybe a couple of auction houses what type of lab report they would want on a diamond if you were to sell it to them. When sellers buy gemstones, they tend to want a report from a lab known for strict grading. When they sell, they sometimes want their stones graded by a lab known for lenient grading and/or minimal information, if their customers don't specify what type of report they want.

A true diamond grading report is not an appraisal and does not have a value or price indicated on the report. It's simply an independent report that identifies and describes an unmounted diamond. The moment a report has a price included, it becomes an appraisal.

Perhaps you're wondering why you'd need a lab report when appraisals also provide identification, treatment and quality information. Major laboratories have greater expertise, more sophisticated equipment and more opportunities to examine important gems than the average jeweler, dealer or appraiser. As a result, they're better equipped to detect enhancements and synthetic gems. Now that more and more treated and synthetic diamonds are entering the market, it's increasingly important to get diamond reports from independent labs that conduct research. If you're paying a high, natural-color price for a colored diamond, it's essential that you get a lab report stating the color is of natural origin

Another advantage of having a grading document from a major lab is that their documents usually carry more weight than appraisals when gems are bought and sold. If you plan to sell an expensive gem on the international market or through an auction house such as Christie's or Sotheby's, it should be accompanied by a recent report from an internationally recognized lab.

In addition to the grading certificate, it is advisable to get a separate appraisal report for expensive diamonds after they are mounted in jewelry (see appraisal chapter). Besides being useful for insurance purposes, an appraisal can help verify that the diamond matches the one described in the diamond report. Appraisers offer appraisals on both mounted and unmounted diamonds. However, the GIA, HRD and some other labs will only grade unmounted diamonds. Prongs can hide inclusions and the apparent diamond color can be influenced by the metal surrounding the stone. In addition, accurate color grading requires comparing the diamond side by side with other unmounted diamonds.

Does a Diamond Report Reveal Everything You Need to Know?

The answer is NO! The current diamond reports of major labs don't tell you how brilliant and transparent a diamond is. That's one of the main reasons why you should look at the stone before you purchase it.

Gemologists define the term **brilliance** as the amount of light returned from a gemstone when viewed face-up, and they distinguish it from sparkle which they call **scintillation**. The *Random House Webster's College*

Dictionary defines "brilliant" as "shining brightly, sparkling, glittery: *brilliant jewels.*"

No matter how it's defined, brilliance is a quality resulting from a combination of factors, including cut proportions, polish, transparency, shape, faceting style, color and clarity. Diamond dealers often use the term "life" for this quality.

You don't have to be a gemologist to be able to judge brilliancy. You can evaluate it both with and without magnification, as long as overhead lighting is used. The darkfield (back-lit) lighting used to grade diamonds in microscopes masks diamond brilliance. Subtle differences are best noted when diamonds are compared side by side. Obvious differences in brilliancy can be easily seen even when the stones are mounted in jewelry.

Transparency is a more specific quality than brilliancy. It refers to how clear, cloudy, hazy or opaque a gemstone is. Transparency differences can be seen with the naked eye. Even though clarity and transparency can be interconnected, they are separate qualities. Two diamonds with the same clarity grade can have different transparencies, even in the case of high clarity grades. For example one VS-grade diamond might be slightly cloudy and another may be highly transparent. Strongly cloudy diamonds, however, would normally receive an imperfect grade. The most prized diamonds have a high transparency.

One disadvantage of the GIA diamond grading report is that it doesn't indicate either the pavilion depth percentage or the pavilion angle, one of the most important determinants of diamond brilliance. The GIA grading report only gives the total depth percentage. However, even if a diamond has an acceptable total depth, it could have a deep pavilion and low crown or vice versa. In other words, the GIA report doesn't always reveal if a diamond has a "fish-eye" effect or dark center. So a diamond can be poorly proportioned even when it's accompanied by a GIA lab report stating it has good polish and symmetry. This is another reason why you should not purchase a diamond solely on the basis of a lab report. Obvious proportion differences can often be seen with the naked eye and are easily visible with a 10-power magnifier.

Some other labs, however, do indicate the pavilion depth percentage in their reports; and in the GIA diamond course, students are taught how to calculate and estimate it. Perhaps in the future they may decide to indicate the pavilion depth percentage on their lab reports.

In the fall of 2005, the GIA plans to introduce a new diamond grading report. One of the biggest changes is that the reports will take into account diamond brilliance. Future AGS reports will also factor in brilliance.

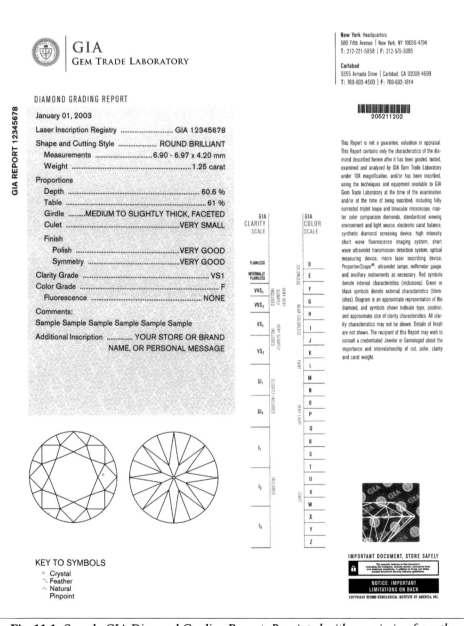

Fig. 11.1 Sample GIA Diamond Grading Report. *Reprinted with permission from the Gemological Institute of America.*

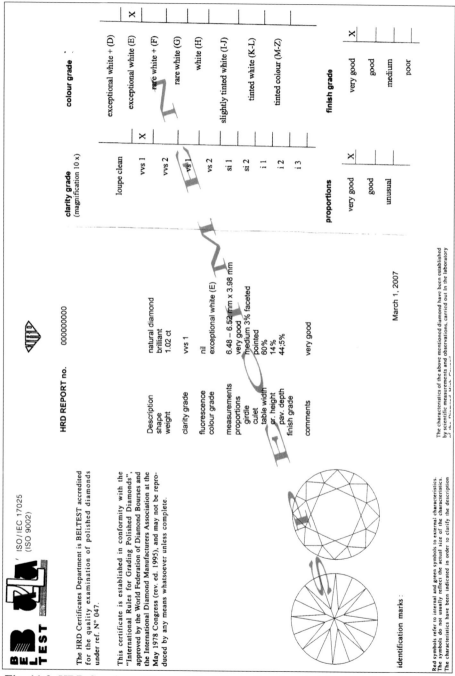

colour grade

exceptional white + (D)	
exceptional white (E)	X
rare white + (F)	
rare white (G)	
white (H)	
slightly tinted white (I-J)	
tinted white (K-L)	
tinted colour (M-Z)	

clarity grade
(magnification 10 x)

loupe clean	
vvs 1	X
vvs 2	
vs 1	
vs 2	
si 1	
si 2	
i 1	
i 2	
i 3	

finish grade

very good	X
good	
medium	
poor	

proportions

very good	X
good	
unusual	

ISO / IEC 17025
(ISO 9002)

The HRD Certificates Department is BELTEST accredited for the quality examination of polished diamonds under ref. N° 047.

This certificate is established in conformity with the "International Rules for Grading Polished Diamonds", approved by the World Federation of Diamond Bourses and the International Diamond Manufacturers Association at the May 1978 Congress (rev. ed. 1995), and may not be reproduced by any means whatsoever unless complete.

HRD REPORT no.   000000000

Description	natural diamond
shape	brilliant
weight	1.02 ct
clarity grade	vvs 1
fluorescence	nil
colour grade	exceptional white (E)
measurements	6.48 – 6.52 mm x 3.98 mm
proportions	very good
girdle	medium 3% faceted
culet	pointed
table width	60%
cr. height	14%
pav. depth	44.5%
finish grade	very good
comments	very good

March 1, 2007

The characteristics of the above mentioned diamond have been established by scientific measurements and observations, carried out in the laboratory

identification marks :

Fig. 11.2 HRD Specimen Diamond Certificate. *Reprinted with permission from HRD (Hoge Raad vorr Diamant).*

Another reason to look at the diamond is to verify that it matches the report. In addition to weights, measurements, and grades, diamond reports have diagrams that map inclusions. The diagrams help differentiate diamonds of the same weight when lab reports become accidentally or intentionally switched.

The most important reason to look at diamonds, rather than relying solely on lab reports is to learn to appreciate their beauty. When you compare high quality diamonds next to mediocre ones, you gain a better understanding of value. A diamond is more than just a set of grades and statistics.

Consumers used to choose diamonds mainly on the basis of emotion. They bought the stones that made them say "Wow! What a gorgeous diamond!" They fell in love with their diamonds just as they did with their sweethearts. Now there's a tendency to go to another extreme and buy diamonds through mail-order or the Internet solely on the basis of a lab report. We need to strike a balance between using our hearts and our minds. We also should realize that our opinion of a diamond is just as important as that of a gem laboratory.

How Important is the Date of a Diamond Report?

For me, the date of a diamond grading report is not very important because I judge diamonds on the basis of their appearance, not on their lab grades. In fact, I'd be willing to buy a diamond with a twenty-year old grading report. Some of the diamonds graded twenty years ago were graded more strictly than they would be today.

If a consumer likes a diamond with an old grading report from a reputable lab, I think it's a better use of money to pay for a thorough appraisal by a qualified independent appraiser than to get another lab report. The appraisal will verify if the lab grades correspond to the current condition of the diamond, and it could serve as a more complete document for insurance purposes because it indicates the value. It could also include details about the mounting.

Some trade members may disagree with me. They argue that lab documents older than six months or a year suggest the diamond isn't desirable enough to have been bought right away. I don't think this a valid objection because diamond dealers typically store lab-graded diamonds individually in safes, not in display cases. If dealers don't have a request for a specific size, shape or quality, the diamond may sit in their safe a long time without ever being viewed. This doesn't mean the diamond is unsaleable.

Even when attractive diamonds are displayed in jewelry stores, there may be no buyers for them, especially in the case of larger diamonds. The customers may not be able to afford the diamonds or the staff may not have good sales skills.

Another claim is that old diamond grading reports do not accurately reflect the quality of a diamond. I don't understand how a diamond's color and clarity can change while it's wrapped in a diamond paper in a safe. If the diamond was previously worn in a mounting, the grade could change, but this is visible when the buyer or appraiser examines the diamond. There are enough factors of concern for a consumer without having to worry about the date of the diamond report. It's more important that the lab report originate from a lab that is not affiliated with or run by the seller.

Mini-certs

Several labs offer shortened versions of their full grading reports. Diagrams of clarity features are not normally included in these less detailed reports, which are sometimes referred to as mini-certs. The GIA calls their brief report the GIA Diamond Dossier. The HRD calls it the HRD Diamond Identification Report.

Some mini-certs indicate the shape, weight, color and clarity of a diamond without giving any details about its proportions, polish or symmetry. To a consumer it might appear that the 4 C's of cut, carat weight, color and clarity are all included. However, shape is a separate price factor from cut quality, which includes the proportioning and finish qualities of the diamond. If a diamond is poorly proportioned, it's not good quality, even if its color and clarity grades are high. Don't be misled into thinking that the cut of a diamond is just its shape.

Mini-certs have the advantage of costing less than full reports, and they can normally be processed quicker. More often than not, they are issued for diamonds weighing less than one carat. For fine quality diamonds of a carat or more, it's advisable to have a full report because it offers you more protection and information.

How Reproducible are Lab Grades?

Some consumers assume that the grades on lab reports are absolute and exact when in fact color and clarity grades are highly subjective. This is one reason major labs often have at least three graders examine each diamond, and they never guarantee that their grades are one hundred per cent accurate.

Most of the time gemologists agree on the grades. However it's not uncommon for color or clarity to fall on a transition point between two grade ranges. In these cases, the majority of the labs assign only one grade per category, and invariably they give the stone the higher grade. A few labs give split grades or place an asterisk next to the grade indicating that it is borderline.

This means that grades are not always reproducible. If you were to resubmit certain diamonds to the same lab for a grade and they were unable to look it up in their data base under the number inscribed on the girdle, the stone could receive a different grade the second time. Because of this, the gem trade accepts a tolerance of plus or minus one grade.

If you were to resubmit the same diamond to different labs, there's an even greater chance that there could be a difference in grades. A difference of two grades or more would indicate that there's a problem with one of the labs. The lab with the higher grades might be catering to retailers or manufacturers who send them a lot of stones for grading. Lab documents are used to sell stones; and the higher the grade, the more the seller can ask for the stone or the better deal the customers think they are getting.

This underscores one of the main themes of this book: you should base your choice of diamond on its appearance, not just on its grading report. If you don't visually examine diamonds before you buy them and compare them side by side with other diamonds, you're asking to get manipulated and ripped off.

You don't have to be a gemologist to see the difference between an SI_1 diamond and one that has a clarity grade of I_1. There are lots of jewelers who will show you how to spot major differences of clarity under a microscope or with a loupe. They can also show you how color and cut quality are evaluated.

Some differences of color and clarity are hard for consumers to see— for example, an IF versus a VVS_2 clarity or a D versus F color. Because of their higher cost, diamonds with grades this high usually warrant being sent to an appraiser who is not connected to the seller or the lab that issued the grading report. Before showing the appraiser the diamond report, ask the appraiser to grade the stone and afterwards compare the grades. This can help you determine if you have a borderline stone or a diamond with inflated grades, or it can give you assurance that the stone was correctly represented to you. Second opinions can be beneficial.

If a diamond has been misrepresented, you may still want to buy it if you selected it because of its appearance. In this case, you should bargain down the price. Otherwise, try to find a similar diamond elsewhere.

When you get a grading report from a gem laboratory, keep in mind that the document is not necessarily the last word. It is at best an independent expert opinion.

Addresses of Some Diamond Grading Labs

Listed below are some of the better known diamond grading laboratories:

AGL (American Gemological Laboratories, Inc.) (founded 1977)
580 Fifth Ave. Suite 706, New York, NY 10036
Phone (212) 704-0727, Fax (212) 764-7614, e-mail: aglgemlab@aol.com
Specializes in colored diamond and colored gem reports, and diamond verification

AIGS (Asian Institute of Gemological Sciences) (founded 1978)
Jewelry Trade Center, 6th floor, 919 Silom Road
Bangkok 10500, Thailand, www.aigsthailand.com
Phone (662) 267-4325/7, Fax (662) 267-4327.

AGSL (American Gem Society Laboratories) (only for the trade)
8917 W. Sahara Ave., Las Vegas, NV 89117
Phone (702) 255-6500, Fax (702) 255-7420, www.agslab.com
Their reports are often used for "ideal-cut" diamonds because the reports include a cut grade based on American "ideal cut" proportions

CCIP Gemological Laboratory (Chambre de Commerce et d'Industrie de Paris Laboratory, also called the French Gemological Laboratory)
2 Place de la Bourse, 75002 Paris, France,
Phone (33) 1 40 26 25 45, Fax (33) 1 40 26 06 75, www.diamants.ccip.fr

CGL (Central Gem Laboratory) (founded 1970)
Miyagi Building, 5-15-14 Ueno, Taito-ku,
Tokyo 110-0005, Japan
Phone (81) 3 3836-1627, Fax (81) 3 3836-6861, www.cgl.co.jp

DEL (Deutsch Diamant und Edelsteinlaboratorien Idar-Oberstein)
(German Diamond and Gemstone Laboratories Idar-Oberstein)
Mainzer Str. 34, D-55743 Idar-Oberstein, Germany
Phone (49) 6781-981355, Fax (49) 6781-981357, www.gemcertificate.com

EGL (European Gemological Laboratory), www.egl.co.za
branches in Antwerp, Johannesburg, Istanbul, London, Tel Aviv and Seoul

EGL USA Group, 6 West 48th Street, New York, NY 10036
(212)-730-7380, Fax (212)-730-7453, www.eglusa.com (founded 1986)
branches in Los Angeles, Vancouver & Toronto. The EGL USA Group is
independent of EGL labs outside of North America

GCAL (Gem Certification and Appraisal Lab)
580 Fifth Avenue, Lower Lobby
New York, NY 10036
Phone (212) 869-8985, Fax (212) 869-2315, www.gemfacts.com

**Gem A (Gemmological Association and Gem Testing Laboratory of
Great Britain)** (only for the trade) (founded 1925)
27 Greville Street, London EC1N 8TN, UK
Phone 44 (207) 404-3334, Fax 44 (207) 404-8843, www.gagtl.ac.uk

GIA Gem Trade Laboratory Inc. (only for the trade) (founded 1949)
5355 Armada Drive, Carlsbad, CA 92008
Phone (800) 421-7250 & (760) 603-4500, www.gia.org
580 Fifth Ave., New York, NY 10036, (212) 221-5858

GGL (Gübelin Gem Lab Ltd)
Maihofstrasse 102, CH-6000 Lucerne 9 / Switzerland
Phone (41) 41 429 1717, Fax (41) 41 429 1734, www.gubelinlab.com

GIT (Gem & Jewelry Institute of Thailand)
Chulalongkorn University, Phayathai University
Phayathai Road, Patumwan
Bangkok 10330 Thailand
Phone (662) 218-5470-4, Fax (662) 218-5474, www.git.or.th

HRD (Hoge Raad vorr Diamant) (founded 1976)
Hoveniersstraat, 22, B-2018 Antwerp, Belgium
Phone (32) 3 222 06 31, Fax (32) 3 222 06 05, www.hrd.be
A branch will open in New York in 2005

IGI (International Gemological Institute) (founded in Antwerp in 1975)
589 Fifth Avenue, New York, NY 10017
(212) 753-7100, Fax (212) 753-7759, www.igiworldwide.com
branches in Antwerp, Bangkok, Cavalese, Dubai, Los Angeles, Mumbai,
Seoul, Tel Aviv, Tokyo, and Toronto

PGS (**Professional Gem Sciences**) (founded 1980)
5 South Wabash, Suite 1905, Chicago IL 60603
(312) 920-1541, (888) 292-1888, Fax (312) 920-1547, www.progem.com

SSEF (Swiss Foundation for the Research of Gemstones) (founded 1974)
Falknerstrasse 9, CH-4001, Basel, Switzerland
Phone (41) 61 262-0640, Fax (41) 61 262-0641, www.ssef.ch

12

Appraisals

"Estimated Retail Replacement Cost: $5000"

On an insurance appraisal, a statement like the one above refers to the retail cost of replacing a piece. It does not mean that the owner of the item can resell it for $5000. By contrast, a liquidation appraisal is the type that gives the immediate cash value of jewelry. You can usually get verbal estimates of the liquidation value free of charge by asking potential buyers and sellers what a stone or jewelry piece is worth. But be aware that the price they offer you can be lower than what you might obtain in a more competitive market such as an auction. Appraisals may also provide values for the purposes of charity donations and estate tax and distribution.

This chapter deals primarily with insurance appraisals because that's the most common appraisal people need.

How is the Retail Replacement Cost Determined?

Since I don't appraise jewelry, I decided to ask three professional appraisers how they determine values for their insurance appraisals. The first appraiser I talked to was **Charles Carmona** in downtown Los Angeles. I first met him when we served as officers for the local GIA Alumni Association. Charles said he determines the cost by first asking clients where they buy their jewelry; he then appraises the piece for the type of store they shop in.

If, for example, the customer regularly shops in the downtown jewelry district where overheads are lower and competition is greater, he will assign a lower retail replacement cost than if they regularly shop in a suburban jewelry store where more services are offered and the overhead is greater. He explains to his clients why a similar piece of jewelry sells for different prices depending where they shop, and the value of extra services and convenience.

Charles says it's best not to value jewelry for more than what customers pay because the higher the appraisal value, the higher their insurance premium. In America, if your jewelry is lost, stolen or damaged, it's unlikely you'll get cash. The insurance company will usually just replace it with a piece matching the description on your appraisal, and they'll buy the piece at wholesale from one of their suppliers.

Charles knows of only one American company that will insure your jewelry by itself for cash—Jewelers Mutual Insurance Company (www.jewelersmutual.com). Other companies require that an expensive piece of jewelry be insured separately as an addendum to your homeowners or renters policy. An **agreed value policy** is available from selected companies (e.g. www.chubb.com)–they will pay you the insured value for a loss, but your premium will be higher for this option.

Charles uses a combination **cost approach** and **market data approach** for appraisals of modern generic jewelry. This means he estimates the cost to manufacture the piece (cost approach) and then applies the appropriate retail mark-up for its market (market data approach).

Properly hallmarked designer pieces (names or stores that are well-known) are appraised at what they are priced to sell for in authorized retail stores (market data approach), and not as generic copies.

Period pieces (i.e., Georgian, Victorian, Edwardian, Art Nouveau, Art Deco, Retro), and especially signed pieces, often sell for more than their intrinsic value and must be compared to sales of similar items at stores that sell estate jewelry, antique shows and auctions (market data approach).

Charles advises his clients to be wary of jewelers who sell their jewelry for one price and give you an insurance appraisal for a higher price. He says they normally sell it for what it's worth, not half of what it's worth.

The second appraiser I interviewed was **Sindi Schloss** in Scottsdale, Arizona. She's a long-time friend whom I met through a jeweler in Phoenix. Like Charles, Sindi bases the retail replacement cost on the most appropriate market in which the jewelry is purchased. If, for example, it's from a designer jewelry store, she will price it in that arena.

If a diamond in a ring is accompanied by a grading report, Sindi does not want to know the grades beforehand, nor the price of the ring. She believes it's her job to independently determine if the price is fair. Ideally the appraisal won't be over valued, yet will provide adequate insurance coverage for 5–7 years, at which time many insurance companies require an update.

According to Sindi, when a diamond is mounted, limitations exist which can make the determination of carat weight and color grade very difficult. When Sindi is grading a mounted diamond, she often gives a triple split color grade with the value based upon the center grade. There are discussions in the professional appraiser world concerning giving a split grade to mounted diamonds. Some appraisers argue that in the event of a loss, an insurance company might replace a diamond that was given a split grade with any of the two or three grades given and often the *lowest* grade. Sindi tries to prevent this by describing that value is based upon the center grade in a cover letter. It's ideal, of course, if the diamond is brought in loose before it is mounted. This removes all the limitations of a mounting and allows an accurate grade. After the diamond is mounted, Sindi finishes the written appraisal and verifies that the diamond is the same and unbroken. (Insurance companies normally don't want to insure loose diamonds because it's too easy to lose them.)

Even if a diamond is accompanied by a report, she prefers to evaluate the diamond before seeing the grade on the report. If the report is from the GIA and she graded it differently by one grade, she'll usually honor the GIA grade, after verifying that it is the same diamond. Sindi doesn't use the SI_3 clarity grade on her appraisals because it is not part of the GIA grading system. An important part of her report is the cover letter in which she explains the market, methodology and value determinants used for the appraisal.

Since many of the items she appraises are purchased from small independent retail jewelry stores, Sindi often uses a combination of the market approach and the cost approach to determine value. For jewelry purchased from well established, multiple outlet retail jewelry stores, typical of those found in malls, she often uses the market data approach; for custom pieces, she'll frequently use the cost approach.

Sindi has the following comments for consumers:

◆ Keep in mind that grading is subjective. Strict graders may grade tougher than an accompanying certificate. There are few graders who strongly dispute a GIA grading report, unless the diamond does not match the plot (map of the inclusions).

◆ Verify that stones match the certificates that they accompany by going to an unbiased, independent appraiser.

The third appraiser I interviewed was **Jennifer Thornton-Davis** in Encino, California. I met her several years ago at a GIA alumni meeting and I see her every February at the Accredited Gemologists Association Conference in Tucson. When Jennifer does a jewelry appraisal, she first researches the **mode**: the market in which the most sales for an item of like, kind and quality occur. She can often determine the type of store in which a diamond ring was purchased by the level of quality in manufacturing and the quality of the stone. Jennifer uses this sales comparison method for most of her appraisals, and she includes a written explanation of how value is developed.

Jennifer says that most people continue to buy diamond rings in traditional jewelry stores. Only about four to five per cent of her clients have bought diamonds on the Internet, and after their purchase, they have her verify the quality. Then when the diamond is mounted, they request a written appraisal of the entire ring to present to their insurance carrier.

If you're purchasing a diamond weighing a carat or more, Jennifer suggests that you consider making sure it's accompanied by a recognized independent lab report. She says she can expect consistent grading from the GIA Gem Trade Lab and the American Gem Society Lab (AGSL). However, with the proliferation of new labs, there can be different grading opinions. Some labs, for example, appear to exist only for the benefit of the seller. Therefore don't assume that just because a lab is independent, it's good. If in doubt, have expensive stones checked by an independent educated gemologist/appraiser. Jennifer advises consumers to ask appraisers about their qualifications, experience and continuing education.

Independent Appraisers versus Jewelry Store Appraisers

Most consumers get their jewelry appraised in jewelry stores because it's convenient and it's a logical place to find a jewelry appraiser. If you trust the jeweler and you don't need a second opinion about the price or quality, this could be good option for you, provided that the store appraiser is well qualified.

The number of independent appraisers is growing because there is increased demand for unbiased jewelry evaluation, especially with the rise in television shopping and Internet sales. Sellers and courts are more likely to honor the opinions of an independent appraiser because conflict of interest is not an issue.

It's easier for independent appraisers to be objective about their valuations because they won't lose a sale if they say a piece is over-priced. In addition, full-time independents get more experience appraising than store appraisers who have to also wait on clients.

Jewelry store appraisers respond by saying they have more experience buying and selling, so they understand the market better and have more contacts for price information. In addition, they may be able to charge less for appraisals since they are profiting from the sale of the appraised merchandise.

Even though it's true that some appraisers are deficient in their knowledge of market valuation, many others have years of prior trade experience and an excellent knowledge of the market. Some have owned jewelry stores, some have been in charge of jewelry auctions, and others have worked as bench jewelers, buyers, sales reps and/or sales associates. Independent appraisers also attend the major gem and jewelry shows and conventions to keep up with prices and to network with buyers and sellers.

The fact is, jewelry store appraisers and independent appraisers can be equally competent in their appraisal skills and knowledge of market values. Choose the type of appraiser that best fits your needs and make sure he or she has high qualifications.

How to Find a Qualified Independent Appraiser

Finding an independent jewelry appraiser can be difficult. Since readers have asked for recommendations, I have added a page to my website that lists independent appraisers who are gemologists with formal appraisal training and accreditation. To see this list of jewelry appraisers go to:

http://reneenewman.com/appraisers.htm

To find appraisers who work either in jewelry stores or independently, go to:

http://www.appraisersassoc.org

http://www.appraisers.org

http://www.isa-appraisers.org

http://www.NAJAappraisers.com

You can also find appraisers if you phone, write, fax or e-mail an appraisal organization and ask for the names of qualified members in your area. Listed below and on the next page are some organizations that will give you the names of appraisers who are members.

In the USA

American Association of Appraisers (AAA)
386 Park Avenue South, Suite 2000, New York, NY 10016
Phone (212) 889-5404, Fax (212) 889-5503
http://www.appraisersassoc.org

American Gem Society (AGS)
8881 West Sahara Avenue, Las Vegas, NV 89117
Phone (702) 255-6500, Fax (702) 255-7420
http://www.ags.org

American Society of Appraisers (ASA)
555 Herndon Parkway, Suite 125, Herndon, VA 20170
Phone (800) ASA-VALU, (703) 478-2228, Fax (703) 742-8471
http://www.appraisers.org

International Society of Appraisers (ISA)
1131 SW 7th St, Suite 105, Renton, WA 98055-1215
Phone (888) 472-4732, (206) 241-0359, Fax (206) 241-0436
http://www.isa-appraisers.org

National Association of Jewelry Appraisers (NAJA)
P. O. Box 18, Rego Park, NY 11374-0018
Phone (718) 896-1536, Fax (718) 997-9057
http://www.NAJAappraisers.org

Canada

Canadian Jeweller's Institute (CJA)
27 Queen St. East, Toronto, Ontario M5C 2M6 Canada
Phone (416) 368-7616 ext 223, Fax (416) 368-1986
http://www.canadianjewellers.com/html/aapmemberlist.htm

Australia

NCJV Inc. (National Council of Jewelry Valuers)
New South Wales Division, Level 10, Dymocks Building
428 George Street, Sydney, NSW 2000 Australia
Phone 02 9232 6599, Fax 02 9232 6399

NCJV Inc. (Victoria Division), 9th Floor
10-16 Queen Street, Melbourne, VIC 3000
Phone 03 9614 3920, Fax 03 9629 2904

NCJV Inc. (Queensland)
Post Office Box 178
Grange, QLD 4051
Phone/Fax 07 3857 4377

NCJV Inc. (South Australia Division)
136 Greenhill Road, Unley, SA 5061
Phone 08 8300 0182, Fax 08 8300 0001

NCJV Inc. (Western Australia Division)
PO Box 501, Wembley, WA 6913
Phone/Fax 08 9409 2009

NCJV Inc.(Tasmania Division)
Post Office Box 13, Barhurst Street Post Office
Hobart, TAS 7000
Phone/Fax 03 6228 3937

After you find the names of some appraisers, you should interview them to find out if they're qualified to appraise your jewelry. When interviewing an appraiser you should ask:

♦ What are your qualifications?
♦ How much do you charge?
♦ What does your appraisal fee include?

Qualifications to Look For

Knowing how to identify gems and gem treatments is essential to accurate appraising. Competent professional appraisers should have one of the following gemological diplomas to prove they've gained the required education needed to identify gemstones.

♦ **AG (CIG)**, Accredited Gemmologist (Awarded by the Canadian Institute Gemmology)
♦ **FCGmA**, Fellow of the Canadian Gemmological Association
♦ **FGA**, Fellow of the Gemmological Association of Great Britain
♦ **FGAA,** Fellow of the Gemmological Association of Australia
♦ **FGG,** Fellow of the German Gemmological Association
♦ **GG**, Graduate Gemologist (Awarded by the Gemological Institute of America)
♦ A gemologist diploma from another school or association, equivalent in stature to those listed above.

Although the gemologist diplomas listed above are important, they don't in themselves qualify people to be appraisers. Appraisers must also be skilled in valuation theory: they must be familiar with gem prices, jewelry manufacturing costs, and the legal aspects of appraising. Appraisers must have trade experience, integrity, and the initiative to keep up with the market and new developments in valuation theory and gemology.

This means appraisers should have taken appraisal courses and performed appraisal work after getting their gemologist diplomas. They should have also had experience working for a jewelry store, a wholesale firm or an auction house. Some of the titles awarded to appraisers are:

♦ **AA-CJI,** Accredited Appraiser of the Canadian Jewellers Institute. Must have a gemologist diploma, a gem lab or access to a lab, 3 years Canadian trade experience, must complete an appraisal course and pass a written and practical exam.

♦ **ASA,** Accredited Senior Appraiser of ASA (the American Society of Appraisers). Must pass an ethics and appraisal exam, submit sample appraisals for peer review, be an accredited member of ASA and have a minimum of five years of full-time appraisal experience.

◆ **CAPP,** Certified Appraiser of Personal Property. This is the highest award offered by the International Society of Appraisers. To receive it, one must attend their appraisal courses, pass the exams, and have a gemological diploma and trade experience.

◆ **CGA,** Certified Gemologist Appraiser. This is awarded by the American Gem Society to certified gemologists who pass their written and practical appraisal exam. Trade experience is a prerequisite.

◆ **CMA,** Certified Master Appraiser. This is the highest award offered by the National Association of Jewelry Appraisers. To receive it, one must have at least seven years of appraisal experience, take the NAJA appraisal studies course, pass a comprehensive theory and practical appraisal examination, and have a NAJA or AGA Certified Gem Laboratory.

◆ **CSM,** Certified Senior Member of the (NAJA). Must have a graduate gemologist diploma, at least five years of trade and appraisal experience, at least 14 days of appraisal training and must pass an appraisal exam.

◆ **MGA,** Master Gemologist Appraiser. This is the highest award offered by the American Society of Appraisers. To receive it, a person must complete the MGA course, pass the MGA tests and have a gemologist diploma, an accredited ASA gem lab, and at least 3 to 5 years appraisal experience.

◆ **ISA,** International Society of Appraisers Accredited Member. Must pass an ethics and appraisal exam, submit sample appraisals for peer review, and have two years of full-time appraisal experience and a college degree or equivalent.

Besides telling you about their educational background and titles, appraisers should also discuss their trade experience and the type of jewelry and gems they usually appraise.

Appraisal Fees

As a consumer, you have the right to know in advance the approximate cost of an appraisal. Occasionally, an appraiser will tell a caller that it's unethical or unprofessional to quote prices over the phone. This isn't true. Professional appraisers should at least be able to tell you their hourly fee and/or their minimum charge if they have one. Some will tell you a flat or approximate appraisal charge for the piece when you describe it to them over the phone. However, in fairness to the appraiser, they are entitled to change their estimate upon seeing the piece if you have played down certain areas of difficulty or have not described it fully.

Some people will offer to appraise your jewelry free of charge, even if you haven't bought it from them. This is a sign that either they want to buy the jewelry from you or else they want to lure you into their store to sell you some of their merchandise. Professionals charge for their services, whether they be lawyers, doctors, accountants or appraisers.

Appraisal fees are charged in a variety of ways. Some are listed below:

♦ A flat fee per item, sometimes a lower fee for each additional piece brought in at the same time
♦ An hourly rate (often combined with a minimum fee)
♦ A rate fully or partly based on the gemstone type
♦ A rate based on the type of report you're seeking, based on the degree of work required.
♦ A percentage rate of the appraised value of your jewelry. The higher the value, the more money the appraiser earns. If you want an appraisal that is as objective as possible, avoid appraisers with this type of fee structure. This is an unethical fee if the appraiser is a member of any of the associations listed previously. The Internal Revenue Service doesn't recognize appraisals done by people who charge percentage fees.

What Does the Insurance Appraisal Include?

The key service the appraiser will provide to you is an accurate, detailed, word picture of the item you're having appraised. The structure of the resulting report will tell you something about the quality of the appraiser's work, and it will help you to better compare appraisal fees. It's understandable that a five-page report with a photo will cost more than one with only a two-sentence description and an appraised value, and you should avoid the latter type. Items that professional independent appraisers normally include with their reports are:

♦ The identity of the stone(s) and metal(s)
♦ The measurements and estimated weights of the stones. (If you can tell appraisers the exact weight of the stones, this will help them give you a more accurate appraisal. Therefore, when buying jewelry, ask stores to write on the receipt any stone weights listed on the sales tags).

◆ Relevant treatment information
◆ A description of the color, clarity, transparency, shape, cutting style, and cut quality of the stones. The grading and color reference system used should also be indicated. Appraisers use different color communication systems to denote color. Four of the best known ones are GemDialogue, AGL Color/Scan, GIA GemSet and Munsell.
◆ Plots of the inclusions in the stones (of either all or only the major stones)
◆ A test of the fineness of the metals
◆ Approximate weight and description of the mounting
◆ The name(s) of the manufacturers or designers of the piece when this is known
◆ A cleaning and inspection of the piece
◆ A photograph
◆ A list of the tests performed and the instruments used.
◆ Definitions or explanations of the terminology used on the report
◆ A biographical sketch of the appraiser's credentials
◆ A Certification of Appraisal Practices sheet (a written code of business ethics for appraisers)

On rare occasions, a country of origin report may also be included, but this requires a high level of expertise.

Suppose you ask someone what their appraisal fee includes and they start specifying a few of the items above. You then ask someone else and they reply, "The value and a description of the piece. What more do you expect?" Haven't those two answers helped you determine who is more qualified to appraise your jewelry?

Besides knowing what appraisers' fees include, you should know what their appraisals look like. Have them show you a sample, and check it for thoroughness and professionalism.

Appraising Jewelry While you Wait

Not all appraisers have a policy of appraising jewelry while you wait. However, it may be inconvenient for you to make two separate trips for an appraisal—one to drop off the jewelry and one to pick it up. Most appraisers will try to accommodate your needs. Some appraisers will only appraise it in front of you. However, they often send you the final written appraisal afterwards. No matter what their policy, you usually need to make an appointment.

Even if it doesn't matter to you whether you leave the jewelry with them or not, it's not a bad idea to ask appraisers if they do on-the-spot appraisals. Their answers will give you added information about them. For example, look at the four responses below. These are actual answers to the question, "Can you do the appraisal on the spot?"

♦ "Only if you pay double because it will keep us off the floor away from selling."

♦ "Yes, but my schedule is limited. What I mostly do is custom design."

♦ "Yes, but it will have to be in the afternoon. I reserve mornings for jewelers and their questions and appraisals."

♦ "No, I need time to analyze the quality of your gemstones and metal work and to do research to arrive at a probative value."

Which of the four are probably most qualified to appraise a $9000 diamond and sapphire ring? Which of the four might be most qualified to appraise custom designed gold jewelry? Which are most likely to give an unbiased appraisal?

Jewelry appraising is an art. There's a lot more to it than simply placing a dollar value on a stone or jewelry piece. If your jewelry has a great deal of monetary value, it's important that you have a detailed, accurate appraisal of it. Take as much care in selecting your appraiser as you did in selecting your jewelry.

13

Branded Diamonds

Finding a well-cut round brilliant is much easier than it used to be. There are many stores now that promote them. Jewelers don't have to order a specific brand in order to get round brilliants of high quality; they only need to deal with suppliers who specialize in well-cut diamonds.

Finding a well-made fancy cut is more difficult. Some jewelers have discovered that they can often save money by buying brand-name fancy-shape diamonds because they don't have to waste money returning poorly made stones, nor do they have to lose time sorting through parcels to find fancy shapes that are well-cut. As a result these jewelers are opting to feature brand-name fancies in their stores. In sum, they like the consistent quality of cut many branded diamonds offer.

Another advantage of some of these branded cuts is that they have distinctive shapes or faceting patterns that attract customers who are looking for something different than the traditional round brilliant.

Brand names are also used to market lab-grown diamonds and treated diamonds in addition to natural diamonds with various color and clarity grades. So whether you buy a branded or a generic diamond, you should verify its quality and ask if it is natural. In other words, judge branded diamonds just as you would any other diamond.

Listed on the following pages are some brands that are not sold exclusively in one retail store or one chain of stores. Their facet patterns are different than that of the standard brilliant cut. These manufacturers don't sell to the general public. However, if you see a cutting style you like, you can find out where it's sold by searching their website or contacting them by phone.

Ashoka®

Ashoka® www.williamgoldberg.com
Patented by William Goldberg Corp in 2002

A modified antique cushion cut with a rectangular girdle outline and rounded corners. It has 62 facets and ranges from D to K color and IF to SI$_2$. Based on the famous diamond of the same name, the Ashoka® is named after the Buddhist warrior-emperor Ashoka Maurya. The English translation of *Ashoka* is "the power to remove sorrow."

Barocut™

Barocut™ www.baroka.com
Patented by Baroka Creations in 2003

Baroka Creations Inc.
New York, NY

Tel: (212) 768-0527, (888) 768-0527
E:mail: info@baroka.com

A rectangular mixed cut referred to as "The Two Heart Diamond" because two hearts are visible meeting point to point at the culet. It has 81 facets and is available in sizes from 20 points and up.

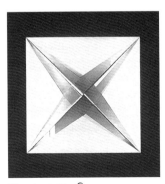

Context Cut®

Context Cut® Wild & Petsch
patented by Dr. Ulrich Freiesleben in 1995
Douglas Mays, Camas, WA (distributor)
Tel: (408) 891-1235

A square octahedral shaped diamond. When viewed from the top, it exhibits a four-pointed, star-shaped diagonal cross. Context cuts® are

expensive to make and are used mostly by high-end designers.

Corona™

Corona™ www.fourever.net
registered by Yuval Harary Diamonds in 2001

Fourever Concept
Ramat Gan, Israel,
Tel: 972 3 575-3111
E-mail: yharary@ netvision.net.il

A square cut with high brilliance. The Corona
has a total of 65 facets, 40 on the pavilion and
25 on the crown. It's available between 0.05
and 2 carats in clarities IF through I_1.

Crisscut®

Crisscut® www.lili-diamonds.com
Patented by Lili Diamonds & Christopher
Designs in 1998
Lili Diamonds (Distributed in the USA by
Christopher Designs Inc.)
Tel: 972 3 575 0011, Ramat Gan, Israel
E-mail: info@ lili-diamonds.com

A step cut with 77 crisscrossed facets and a
rectangular or an octagonal shape. Rectangular
Crisscuts come in calibrated sizes ranging from
0.05 to 20 carats and are used mainly for jewelry, whereas octagonal
Crisscuts ranging in size from 0.15 carats and up are usually sold as
solitaires.

Cushette®

Cushette® Cut www.cushette.com
Patented by Diamco in 2003

A cushion shape with
the brilliance of a round
diamond. It's hand cut
with 33 facets on the
crown and 44 on the

pavilion. Cushettes range in size from 0.25 to
10 carats and are certified by GCAL.

Flanders Ideal Square Cut®

Flanders Ideal Square Cut®
www.nationaldiamond.com

Square brilliant-cut diamond with cut corners and 62 facets, including the culet. Developed in the late 1980's, the Flanders Cut is available in sizes from 0.05 to 5 carats and in clarities of I_1 to IF. It bears the name of the region where it was first polished, the northern Federal Region of Belgium—Flanders.

Gabrielle® cushion cut

Gabrielle® www.gabriellediamonds.com
Patented by Gabriel Tolkowsky/Suberi Bros in 2002.

A "triple brilliant" cut named after its creator, Gabi Tolkowsky. It comes in nine shapes—round, pear, oval, marquise, heart, cushion, shield, octagonal square and octagonal rectangle. Most of the shapes have 105 facets. Gabrielle® diamonds are available in clarities from IF down to I_1 and in sizes 0.10 cts and up.

Jubilant Crown®

Jubilant Crown® www.jcrdiamond.com
Patented by Edwin Bruce Cutshall in 2001

Gem International, manufacturer & distributor
New York, NY
Tel: (212) 840-2111, (800) 840-2112

A modified round brilliant with a smaller table and 16 more crown facets than a traditional round brilliant. Table sizes range from 40 to 45%, and carat weights start at 0.19 carats. The Jubilant Crown® is available in clarities from I_1 and up in D to K colors.

Lily Cut®

Lily Cut® www.lili-diamonds.com

Patented by Lili Diamonds in 1997

Lili Diamonds: main office in Israel and two branches in Hong Kong and New York
E-mail: info@lili-diamonds.com
Tel 972 3 575 0011

A flower shaped diamond with a square table. It has 65 facets and comes in D through M/N colors and in calibrated sizes from 0.20 carats and up. The Lily Cut® is often used in women's rings and earrings in addition to line bracelets.

Lucére® Diamond

Lucére® Diamond www.cutbygauge.com

Cut by Gauge Diamonds
(312) 236-7351,

A mixed-cut, square diamond with cut corners that has a three-tiered, step-cut crown with 25 facets and a modified, brilliant-cut pavilion with 40 facets. Carat weights start at 0.25 carats and table sizes range from 54 to 63%. The Lucére diamond is available with GIA, AGS, or PGS lab reports in clarities of IF to I₁ and in colors D through M.

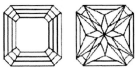

Quadrillion® www.bezambar.com

patented by Ambar Diamonds in 1981

A square diamond with 49 brilliant style facets: 21 crown, 24 pavilion, and 4 girdle facets. When the quadrillion was developed in the early 1980's, it was the first brilliant-style square cut (the original princess cut). Before then, square diamonds were step cut. Bez Ambar has made improvements to the cut and now calls it Quad 2000.

Quadrillion®

Royal Asscher®

Royal Asscher® www.asscher.nl
Patented by Royal Asscher Diamond Co. 2002

Royal Asscher Diamond Company
Tel 31(0) 20 679-1311
E-mail: royal@asscher.nl
Distributed in the US by M. Fabrikant & Sons

A 74-facet modern
Asscher (step-cut
square). See Chapter
9 for more details.

Royal Brilliant®

Royal Brilliant® www.exroyal.com
Patented by Exroyal Co. in 1986

Exroyal Co.Inc.
New York, NY
(212) 371-0007
exroyal@attglobal.net

An 82-facet round brilliant
with 10 double bezel facets
and 10 pavilion mains,
which creates patterns of
ten hearts and ten arrows
instead of the usual eight.

Spirit Diamond®

Spirit Diamond® or **Spirit Sun®**
patented by Dr. Ulrich Freiesleben in 1997

Douglas Mays, US distributor for Wild & Petsch
Camas, WA
Tel: (408) 891-1235

A modern round diamond, which has 16 equal
crown facets and 16 equal pavilion facets rad-
iating outwards. The Spirit Diamond® is most
often used in high-end designer jewelry.

Tiana®

Tiana® www.tianadiamond.com

Britestar Diamond Co. Ltd
New York, NY 10036
Tel: (800) 458-7200, (212) 719-4020
E-mail: info@tianadiamond.com

A modified cushion cut, which is square or rectangular and has 73 facets. Sizes range from 0.50 to 2.5 carats. The Tiana® comes in D to K colors and IF to I_1 clarities. Each diamond is lab graded by either IGI or AAG.

Trielle®

Trielle® www.trilliondiamond.com

Trillion Diamond Company
New York, NY 10036-2802
Tel: (212) 869-7450, (800) TRILLION
E:mail: contact@trilliondiamond.com

An equilateral triangle, brilliant-cut with 50 facets. In 1978 it was patented as the Trillion, but the name was changed to Trielle in1991 because the term "trillion" was being used to refer to any brilliant-cut triangle. Every Trielle diamond from 0.20 on up is cut with identical proportions, so they are fairly easy to match.

Tycoon Cut®

Tycoon Cut® www.tycooncut.com
Patented by Tycoon Jewelry in 2002

A rectangular diamond with 24 facets on the pavilion and nine on the crown. The top center facet is in the shape of a diamond, making it the "only diamond with a diamond on the top." Sizes start at 0.05 carats. Every Tycoon cut above 0.50 carat is accompanied by a GIA diamond grading report.

Virtue Cut®

Virtue Cut® www.doranisaak.com

Doron Isaak Couture Gems
Beverly Hills, CA 90212
(310) 274-3311, info@doranisaak.com

A step-cut diamond shape with 21 facets. Carat weights are 0.20 to 3 carats and clarities are VS and up. Color grades range from D to G and fancy yellow to vivid yellow. Virtue Cuts are featured in designer jewelry, which is sold at very high-end independent retailers.

WebCut®

WebCut® www.thewebcut.com
Patented by the Dali Diamond Co. in 2003

Dali Diamond Company
Antwerp, Belgium, 32 3 233 7941
E-mail: webcut@dalidiamond.com

Designed like a spider's web, the WebCut® has 24 facets on the pavilion and 24 on the crown plus the table. It's available in 0.20 to 3 carats in D to I colors from IF to SI₁. An HRD certificate is included with each WebCut® diamond.

Princette®

Princette Cut® www.varna.com

Mark Silverstein
Woodland Hills, CA
(800) 993-5900

48-facet "princess cut" baguettes. Used mainly as a bridal stone, the Princette® is sold mounted in designer jewelry. It is available in G to D colors and SI₁ to IF clarities. The most popular sizes are 0.10 to 0.20 carats.

14

How to Avoid Ripoffs

One of the best ways to learn how to avoid ripoffs is to listen to the stories of other people who have shopped for diamonds. To illustrate this, I recently talked to two individuals and two couples about their experience of shopping for a diamond engagement ring. Three of the experiences were for the most part positive, but one was negative. Let's begin with the negative true story of a doctor and his wife; let's call them John and Jill. It occurred a few years prior to the publication of this book.

Neither John nor Jill did any research on diamonds before they bought one. Through her job, Jill met a diamond dealer who said he could give them a really good deal on a stone. When it was time to get an engagement diamond, they simply went to his office and purchased one.

Since Jill was quite artistic, she decided to design her own ring. The dealer helped them find a jeweler in a nearby office to make it. When it was time to pick up the ring, it didn't look anything like the various sketches Jill had drawn. She was devastated and ran into the hall sobbing. The jeweler was furious that they didn't like it; he yelled and swore, saying he'd just scrap the ring and they could take their diamond.

John was so stunned by the events that he didn't know what to do. He figured it would be best to talk to the dealer and have him rectify the situation, but the dealer wasn't in his office and never returned his calls. John learned later that the dealer had moved out of town. John was never able to get his diamond back because the jeweler wouldn't answer the door. They ended up buying an engagement ring in a reputable jewelry store and were happy with their final purchase.

John now regrets that he didn't take the diamond immediately when he was at the jeweler's. John isn't sure what kind of diamond they bought from the dealer or if the price was fair. But this is because he didn't know what type of documentation to ask for, and he hadn't done any prior research. Unfortunate experiences like this can be avoided. The purpose of this chapter is to show you how.

Until I heard this story, I hadn't planned on discussing custom-made jewelry because my book, the *Diamond Ring Buying Guide*, dealt with the topic. But since disappointments can occur in these situations, I've decided to briefly list some precautions you should take when jewelers do custom work for you. However, I'd first like to point out some other things John and Jill should have done:

◆ They should have done research and looked at diamonds in jewelry stores before buying one; this would have given them a basis for comparing prices and quality. The fact that the dealer disappeared after the sale suggests he may have misrepresented his diamonds. If John and Jill had known something about diamonds and had asked relevant questions, they probably would have realized beforehand that he was not a good person to do business with.

◆ Before giving the dealer any money, they should have obtained written documentation describing the diamond. They should also have asked for a written work order and a receipt from the jeweler indicating they gave him that diamond. John and Jill were unable to pursue the matter because they had no written proof that the jeweler had their diamond. They couldn't confront the jeweler face to face again because he didn't have a store front. He only had an office with a camera that allowed him to screen all visitors.

◆ Since they had never done business with either the dealer or jeweler, they should have had the diamond checked by an independent appraiser before taking it to the jeweler. He or she could have verified the quality of the diamond and possibly helped them recover their diamond.

◆ Even though they didn't have written documentation, John and Jill should have reported the jeweler to their local better business bureau and to the management office of the building he was in. They should have asked for advice from them and from jewelers' organizations such as:

Jeweler's Vigilance Committee (JVC)
25 W. 45th #400, New York, NY 10036,
(212) 997-2002, www.jvclegal.org

Jewellers Vigilance Canada (JVC)
27 Queen St. E. #600, Toronto, ON M5C 2M6, Canada
(416) 368-4840, (800) 636-9536, www.jewellersvigilance.ca

Precautions to Take When Having Jewelry Custom-made

Jill would have probably had a better experience with custom-made jewelry if she had followed some of the suggestions below.

◆ **Before selecting a jeweler, ask to see some examples of his or her best work.** Normally the quality of the work jewelers will do for you will be no better than what they have done for others. If you're not satisfied with the samples, go someplace else.

◆ **Try on rings that resemble the one you want to have made.** What looks good in a picture may not look or feel good on your hand. Ideally the jeweler who does your work will have some models in your store that are similar to what you want designed. Sometimes custom designers keep a large library of silver rings representing possible ring styles.

◆ **If possible, have good drawings, photos or models of the ring you want made.** Never assume that the jeweler understands your verbal description of what you want.

◆ **Don't assume a ring will look exactly like it does in a photo.** It should, however, have a close resemblance. The best way to get exactly what you want is to have a model or a sample ring. Jill's experience proves this. She had good drawings, but evidently the jeweler didn't understand them.

◆ **Be as specific as possible about ring features that you consider important.** For example, state in advance if you want the prongs holding your diamonds to be rounded off or hammered in a square or triangular form. Otherwise, the jeweler will assume that the prong style doesn't matter to you so long as the prongs are secure and uniform and don't cover too much of the diamonds.

　　You should also tell the jeweler beforehand if you want the inside of your ring to have a special look. In one instance, a lady wanted thin bars under every stone of a diamond eternity band instead of under every other stone. Unless jewelers are told otherwise, they will probably assume that as long as the inside of a ring is smooth and well polished, its appearance won't matter much to a customer since the inside doesn't show when the ring is worn.

◆ **If the ring is being cast, ask to see the wax model before casting**. Point out any areas you think might be problematic, and suggest alterations if needed. Since the wax is fragile, jewelers normally do not let customers try on the wax model. However, once the ring is cast, you should try it on before the stones are set. It's easier to make changes without the stones in the settings.

◆ **If you have a ring that fits well and has about the same band width as the custom ring you are ordering, show it to the jeweler or sales-person so they can choose the best ring size.** The sample metal rings they have you try on can sometimes suggest the wrong size. Some jewelers take your size each time they see you in order to take into account size fluctuations, as in summer versus winter. Some people's finger size even changes during the course of a day.

◆ **Always tell a jeweler you need the ring earlier than you actually do,** especially if it's a complicated job. Work out an acceptable delivery date and have it put in writing. But still be prepared for delays. It's best not to rush custom-made jewelry.

◆ **If possible, avoid having jewelry custom made in December in countries that celebrate Christmas.** Since jewelers are rushed and overworked at that time of year, they might not do their best work.

◆ **Get a written estimate of the cost of the ring.** If more diamonds are needed than estimated, the jeweler is not expected to give them to you free of charge. He should, however, get your permission before doing anything that would increase the estimated cost of the ring. If you leave gemstones with the jeweler, a brief description of them should be indicated on the work order.

◆ **Know in advance who will be responsible if your diamonds are lost or damaged during setting or recutting.** If you give a jeweler your diamonds, he's not always liable if something unfortunate happens to them. Reliable jewelers, however, will either feel morally obligated to replace damaged or lost diamonds, or else will clearly warn you that your diamonds are at risk.

◆ **Know the refund policy of the jeweler.** It's normal for jewelers to retain at least a portion of your deposit if you decide not to buy the ring you ordered, particularly if it's a style that would be difficult to sell. John and Jill didn't have to pay a deposit; it seems that the jeweler considered the diamond as the deposit. Professional jewelers normally require a deposit.

◆ **Develop a relationship with a jeweler you can trust and who looks after your welfare.** Then you won't have to worry about having unpleasant surprises when you have jewelry custom made. In addition, he or she can help you find buys that you wouldn't find on your own.

Custom jeweler Eve Alfillé says that you should expect the following sequence of steps in the custom work process. "You will:
1. Give your order and leave a deposit.
2. Come in to look at a wax model (and/or to view the stones chosen), understanding that the wax model will always look a little "clunky"— it has no reflectivity, and also needs to be a little heavier to allow for shrinkage and polishing.

3. Come in for a size fitting before the stones are set; you get to see your ring, but it probably will not have the final finish and polish. In fact yo u might decide you prefer it matte rather than high polished.
4. Come and get the finished ring, pay the balance, and walk off into the sunset, admiring your glorious new diamond ring."

Three Stories of Satisfied Consumers

A week after John told me about his diamond purchases, I met a lady named Amy. She had studied my book, the *Diamond Ring Buying Guide,* before shopping for an engagement diamond with her future husband. They were both pleased with her diamond and her ring.

Amy spent over four months looking for a diamond in the Los Angeles metropolitan area and found one she liked at a good price downtown in the Los Angeles jewelry district. She said that she was able to use a loupe to make judgments about diamonds, but she made her final selection with the aid of a microscope. I asked her if she had any advice to pass along to consumers. Here are some of her tips:

◆ Don't buy the first diamond you see. Do your homework beforehand and shop around. You can't be too prepared.

◆ Look at the diamonds against a stark white surface. Some stores Amy visited placed the diamond on black velvet or leather, but this would hide the yellowish tint of their diamonds. As soon as the diamond was placed on a white card, the actual color would become more evident.

◆ Choose a diamond and a mounting that will remain in style. Amy saw a lot of trendy styles, but ended up purchasing a round brilliant diamond with a classic style mounting.

◆ Instead of telling salespeople the maximum you can spend,.tell them what type of diamond you are looking for.

◆ Get a cert (diamond grading report) if the diamond is expensive.

◆ Make sure the diamond matches the description on the cert. Amy found one whose inclusions did not match those shown on the accompanying grading report. She pointed this out to the jeweler who acknowledged that it was true. If there is a laser inscription, make sure it is the same as on the report. High magnification (25 power +) is usually required to decipher the numbers on the diamond's girdle.

◆ Don't get caught up in the commercialism of shopping for diamonds. Remember the symbolism of the ring, which has no beginning or end, and wear it as an eternal commitment of your love.

The information that Amy gave me was so useful that I decided to interview two couples I knew, who had read the *Diamond Ring Buying Guide* before their diamond purchase.

The first couple, Steve and Mary, are friends of mine. Originally, Mary wanted a yellow radiant or princess-cut diamond. However, they couldn't get the depth of color and size for the price they wanted, so they decided to look for a colorless round brilliant-cut diamond instead.

Steve said the salespeople were more forthcoming about the quality of their diamonds and were more willing to negotiate when they learned he had knowledge about diamonds, so he advises consumers to do research before shopping.

After visiting several stores and not finding what they wanted, a friend suggested an independent jewelry store in the suburbs, which was owned by a third generation jeweler. Steve and Mary decided to buy an engagement ring from him because he made them feel comfortable, he did not pressure them, he let them compare his diamonds side by side, and he had the prettiest mounting Mary had seen. It was classy and elegant without being too complicated, and it was well made. They bought the center diamond from the same jeweler because they knew he would insure the stone against any possible damage during setting if it was from his store. In addition, he offered a lifetime guarantee on the craftsmanship of the ring and the opportunity to upgrade their diamond at any time. For an additional $200 they could have had a lifetime guarantee covering any damage to the diamond.

Since the engagement ring cost more than expected, they decided to have the diamond wedding band made in the downtown jewelry district where the prices seemed to be cheaper. The band turned out to be acceptable and properly represented. However, Steve and Mary now wish that the first jeweler had made it because when they compare the engagement ring side by side with the band, they can see that the engagement ring is better crafted and the diamonds in it are better matched than in the diamond wedding band. Steve says they paid a price in quality to get the band cheaper. Nevertheless, they are glad they did prior research and did not purchase the first rings they saw.

The second couple I interviewed was Doug and Beth, who were from the Southeastern part of the United States. They started looking at diamond rings casually while they were dating, but when the search became more serious, they focused on finding a knowledgeable jeweler they could trust.

Doug, a distant cousin of mine, told me that whenever he makes a major purchase, he does research on the item. Then he formulates one or two questions that will help him determine if the salespeople are believable. For example, before buying a Toyota, he gathered information and discovered that the model they wanted did not have an outside antenna. So his test question was, "Where's the outside antenna?" Doug didn't mind if salespeople said "I don't know, but I'll find out for you;" but if they made up a wrong answer, they lost his business.

The *Diamond Ring Buying Guide* was Doug's initial source of information on diamonds. After reading it, he decided to ask salespeople to show him diamonds under a microscope. One person responded that a loupe was more powerful than a scope, another person rationalized that "if your human eye can't see the interior of a diamond, what's the point of looking at it under a gem scope." Someone else refused to show them diamonds under the microscope even though there was one in the store.

When a salesperson voluntarily had them look at stones through the gem scope, this increased their trust and made them feel that there was nothing to hide. Doug and Beth found it fascinating to look at diamonds under magnification.

They ultimately bought a solitaire ring at a combination rock shop/jewelry store that specializes in colored gems. Some of the diamonds were loose, others were mounted. Even though the selection of diamonds was smaller than that of other stores they visited; the overall quality was better. Listed below are the reasons Doug and Beth gave for purchasing their diamond at the rock shop:

◆ Nobody in the store was pushy or high-pressured. The salespeople were patient and just let them spend as much time as they wanted looking at diamonds, which made them feel comfortable.

◆ The staff answered their questions effectively.

◆ The owner let them compare four or five diamonds together. Doug and Beth wanted to see at least two stones side by side, but some stores could only show one diamond at a time, citing insurance restrictions.

◆ The owner took Doug and Beth to the back and let them look at their diamonds under the microscope.

◆ The way the jeweler graded diamonds seemed to be stricter than at other stores.

◆ The solitaire ring setting they liked had six prongs. Some places only had settings with four prongs; one salesperson even said there was no difference between a four-prong and a six-prong setting. Doug and Beth never went back to that particular store.

◆ When they asked to see the diamond they liked under natural light, the rock shop/jewelry store owner just took them outside and let them look at it. Beth was surprised at how sparkly the diamond was outside.

Doug understood why other stores couldn't let them see any of their diamonds in daylight, but he said that another jeweler had a room with simulated natural light, and he found that helpful

◆ The store was very accommodating and made it easy to buy a diamond. When Doug said he wanted to think about his selection, the owner replied that he would set it aside for a month and promised that he could find any diamond Doug or Beth might want.

Two weeks later Doug called the owner and said he wanted the diamond. He not only returned to buy the diamond ring, but has gone back over the past five years and purchased several gifts for Beth, including two pendants, two pairs of earrings, a necklace, a tennis bracelet and a scarab bracelet. Doug's goal is to have a good shopping experience whenever he makes a purchase. With respect to jewelry, he's achieved that.

More Tips on Smart Buying

Amy, Steve & Mary, and Doug & Beth had different buying experiences, but all of them are pleased with their engagement ring purchases. These positive results did not occur just by chance. Here are more guidelines that helped them and can help you.

◆ **When judging prices, try to compare diamonds of the same shape, size, color, clarity and cut quality**. Compare mountings with the same metal type, weight, setting styles and workmanship. All of these factors affect the cost of a diamond ring. Because of the complexity of jewelry pricing, it's easiest for a lay person to compare diamonds or rings that are similar.

◆ **Compare per-carat diamond prices, not stone prices** (total cost of a diamond). Dealers calculate diamond prices by multiplying the carat weight times the price per carat. See Chapter 2.

◆ **Ask if the diamond(s) is untreated and natural.** A salesperson who claims a diamond is untreated should be willing to identify it as an untreated natural diamond on the sales receipt. Make this a condition of sale. If a salesperson says a diamond is enhanced or processed, then it's treated.

In some instances, you can save a lot of money by buying treated diamonds. However, for something as special as a wedding ring, it's advisable to get an untreated diamond, but that is a decision the buyer will have to make.

If a jeweler or salesperson tells you they don't know if a diamond is treated, this is not a sign of incompetence—it's an indication of honesty. Treatments are now so sophisticated that trade members can't always be expected to be able to identify them. Jewelers usually assure themselves that their diamonds are untreated by sending them to specialized labs for examination and/or by purchasing them from sources that guarantee they're untreated.

◆ **Don't assume that all jewelers grade diamonds in the same way.** Some jewelers are more strict than others, so grades can be misleading. That's why it's important for you to understand how to judge diamond quality and to look at diamonds under magnification before buying them. Even diamonds accompanied by grading reports or certificates should be viewed carefully by the buyer. Many of these written evaluations, even from reputable labs, do not give a good description of the quality of the cut or the degree of brilliance. In addition, some labs have stricter grading standards than others.

◆ **Beware of sales or ads that seem too good to be true.** The advertised merchandise might be of unacceptable quality or it might have been stolen or misrepresented. Jewelers are in business to make money, not to lose it.

◆ **Be willing to compromise.** Like Steve and Mary, you may have to do this in order to find a good buy and stay within your budget. Even people with unlimited budgets have to compromise sometimes on the size, shape, color or quality they want because of lack of availability. It's especially difficult to find natural fancy-color diamonds of specific qualities, cuts and sizes. A diamond doesn't have to be perfect for you to enjoy it.

◆ **Make sure expensive diamonds are accompanied by a lab report.** It's not worth buying a lab report for a $300 diamond, but it is for a $3000 diamond. A lab report offers an independent assessment of the color, clarity and proportions of the stone, and it can protect you from ending up with a synthetic or treated diamond. For information on gem labs, appraisals and lab reports, consult Chapters 11 and 12.

◆ **Look at the diamond(s) on your hand as it (they)would normally be viewed** and answer the following questions. (A negative answer to any one of the questions suggests the diamond is a poor choice).
   a. Is the diamond brilliant?
   b. Does it sparkle?

    c. Does it look good compared to other diamonds of the same shape and size? Bear in mind that lighting can affect the appearance of diamonds, so try to view them under different lights—fluorescent, daylight, spotlights, light bulbs and away from light.

◆ Put the ring on your finger and answer the following questions. (Again, a negative answer suggests the ring is a poor choice).
    a. Does it look good on your hand?
    b. Does it feel good on your hand?
    c. Is there a good chance that it will stay in style?
    d. Does it fit your personality?
    e. Is it practical for how you plan to wear it?

You might have expected the *Diamond Handbook* to tell you what types of diamonds are best and where the best places are to buy them. The fact is, however, there is no one diamond or jeweler for all people. Choosing a diamond ring and jeweler is a personal matter. The *Diamond Handbook* was written to help you make your own buying decisions, not to dictate what you should buy.

When you purchase a diamond ring, you're getting more than just a rock attached to a hunk of metal. You're getting a work of art that you can hold and wear. You're getting a symbol of beauty, purity, strength and eternity. These symbolic associations are the result of the intrinsic characteristics of the ring materials.

Gold, platinum and diamonds have a lot in common. In their pure state, they're all composed of a single atomic element; they're all chemically stable and will not tarnish or change with time; they can all be used as ornaments or as a medium of exchange; they're all important to the health and welfare of modern man because of their technical and industrial applications; they've all played an important role in the history of mankind.

Before the 1700's, only kings, queens and other nobility were allowed to wear diamond jewelry. This is no longer an exclusive privilege. You can have the pleasure of wearing diamonds and giving them as pledges of love and commitment. Your diamond jewelry is very special, just like the person wearing it. So treasure it; take good care of it. If you do, it can bring you and your loved ones years of enjoyment.

Appendix

The information below is based mostly on the following sources:

Gems by Robert Webster

GIA Gem Reference Guide

Handbook of Gem Identification by Richard Liddicoat

Chemical, Physical & Optical Characteristics of Diamonds

Chemical composition: C, Crystallized carbon

Mohs hardness: 10

Specific gravity: 3.52 (±.01)

Toughness: Good in cleavage directions, exceptional in other directions

Cleavage: Perfect in four directions

Fracture: Step-like

Streak: White

Crystal system: Cubic

Crystal descriptions: Mainly octahedrons, also cubes, rhombic dodecahedrons, twins and plates

Optic Character: Singly refractive

Refractive Index: 2.417

Birefringence: None

Dispersion: .044

Luster: Adamantine

Pleochroism: None

UV fluorescence: Inert to strong, usually blue (LW), weaker (SW)
See Chapter 6 for more details

Reaction to chemicals: None

Stability to light: Stable

Reaction to heat:
   Begins to vaporize in an oxygen-rich atmosphere at 690°C to 875°C

Absorption spectra:
   415.5 nm: strongest absorption line in cape series
   504 nm: prominent line in brown and greenish yellow diamonds
   594 nm: thin line in natural-color diamonds from China and irradiated
   and annealed diamonds, when cooled to low temperatures

Cause of color:
   Yellow and Orange: Nitrogen and related color centers. Blue: boron
   Green: Color center due to irradiation
   Red, pink, brown: unknown, maybe structural abnormalities

Suppliers of the Diamonds for Photos in This Book

Cover photo: Harry Winston Inc., New York, NY

Inside front cover photos: Top: Joseph DuMouchelle International Auctioneers, Grosse Pointe Farms, MI
Middle: Harry Winston, Inc., New York, NY
Bottom: Gemological Institute of America, Carlsbad, CA

Inside back cover photos: Top: Harry Winston, Inc., New York, NY
Alan Hodgkinson, Portencross by West Kilbride, Ayrshire, Scotland

Title page: Exroyal Co. Inc, New York, NY

Chapter 2
Figs. 2.1 to 2.13, & 2.29: Josam Diamond Trading Corp., Los Angeles, CA
Fig. 2.14: Ernest Slotar, Inc., Chicago, IL
Figs. 2.17, 2.18: J. Landau Inc, Los Angeles, CA

Chapter 3
Fig 3.2: Exroyal Co. Inc, New York, NY
Fig. 3.4: Josam Diamond Trading Corp., Los Angeles, CA
Fig. 3.6: Diamco, New York, NY
Fig. 3.8: Bez Ambar Inc., Los Angeles, CA
Figs. 3.10: 3.12, & 3.16: Josam Diamond Trading Corp., Los Angeles, CA
Fig. 3.14: National Diamond Syndicate, Chicago, IL.
Fig. 3.18: Ernest Slotar, Inc., Chicago, IL
Fig. 3.21: Mark Gronland Custom Jewelry, Umatilla, FL

Chapter 4
Figs. 4.4, 4.11- 4.13: Josam Diamond Trading Corp., Los Angeles, CA
Figs. 4.14, 4.15, 4.16: J Landau, Inc., Los Angeles, CA

Chapter 5

Figs 5.1–5.30: Josam Diamond Trading Corp., Los Angeles, CA

Chapter 9

Figs. 9.1 & 9.2: The Gem Lab, Rochester, NY

Fig. 9.3: Harry Winston Inc., New York, NY

Fig. 9.8 & 9.9: Ebert & Co., Los Angeles, CA

Fig. 9.12: Harry Winston Inc., New York, NY

Fig. 9.16–9.22: The Gem Lab, Rochester, NY

Fig. 9.24: Royal Asscher Diamond Co., Amsterdam

Fig. 9.25: The Gem Lab, Rochester, NY

Fig. 9.30: D & E. Singer, Inc., New York, NY

Fig. 9.41: Joseph DuMouchelle Intl Auctioneers, Grosse Pointe Farms, MI

Bibliography

Diamonds

Balfour, Ian. *Famous Diamonds.* London: William Collins Sons & Co Ltd., 1987.

Blakey, George G. *The Diamond.* London: Paddington Press Ltd., 1977.

Bruton, Eric. *Diamonds.* Radnor, PA: Chilton, 1978.

Cuellar, Fred. *How to Buy a Diamond.* Naperville, IL: Casablanca Press, 2000.

Dickinson, Joan Younger. *The Book of Diamonds.* New York: Crown Publishers, 1965.

Gemological Institute of America. *Diamonds & Diamond Grading* Course, 2002.
Gemological Institute of America. *Diamonds & Diamond Grading* Course 1986.
Gemological Institute of America. *Diamonds* Course 1979.
Gemological Institute of America. *The GIA Diamond Dictionary.* Santa Monica, CA: GIA, 1993.

Harlow, George E. *The Nature of Diamonds.* Cambridge University Press, 1997.

Hofer, Stephen C. *Collecting & Classifying Coloured Diamonds.* New York: Ashland Press, 1998.

Koivula, John. *The Microworld of Diamonds.* Northbrook, IL: Gemworld International Inc., 2000.

Kassoy Inc. *Everything You Always Wanted to Know about Diamonds.* New York: Kassoy Inc., 1977.

Ludel, Leonard. *Recutting & Repairing Diamonds.*1996.

Newman, Renée, *Diamond Ring Buying Guide: How to evaluate, identify, select & care for diamonds & diamond jewelry.* Los Angeles: International Jewelry Publications, 2002.
Newman, Renée, *Diamond Ring Buying Guide: How to Spot Value & Avoid Ripoffs.* Los Angeles: International Jewelry Publications, 1989.
Newman, Renée, *Gem & Jewelry Pocket Guide.* Los Angeles, International Jewelry Publications, 2003.

Pagel-Theisen, Verena. *Diamond Grading ABC.* Antwerp: Rubin & Son, 2001.
Pagel-Theisen, Verena. *Diamond Grading ABC.* New York: Rubin & Son, 1986.

Roskin, Gary. *Photo Masters For Diamond Grading.* Northbrook, IL: Gemworld International, 1994.

Shuster, William George. *Legacy of Leadership: a History of the Gemological Institute of America.* Carlsbad, CA: Gemological Institute of America. 2003.

Spero, Saul A. *Diamonds, Love, & Compatibility.* Hicksville, NY: Exposition Press, 1977.

Vleeschdrager, Eddy. Dureté 10: Le diamant, 3 édition, histoire-taille-commerce. Deurne (Anvers): 1996.

Jewelry and Gems

AGTA, *1997-98 Source Directory* & Gemstone Enhancement Information Chart.

Carmona, Charles. *The Complete Handbook for Gemstone Weight Estimation.* Los Angeles: Gemania Publishing, 1998.

Cologni, Franco & Nussbaum, Eric. *Platinum by Cartier.* Harry N. Abrams. 1996.

Gemological Institute of America. Appraisal Seminar handbook.
Gemological Institute of America. Gem Identification Course.
Gemological Institute of America. Jewelry Repair Workbook.
Gemological Institute of America. Jewelry Sales Course.
Gemological Institute of America. *Gem Reference Guide.* Santa Monica, CA: GIA, 1988.

Geolat, Patti, Van Northrup, C., Federman, David. *The Professional's Guide to Jewelry Insurance Appraising.* Shawnee Mission, KS: Modern Jeweler, 1994.

Gubelin, Eduard & Franz-Xavier, Erni. *Gemstones: Symbols of Beauty and Power.* Lucerne: EMB Service for Publishers, 2000.

Hanneman, Wm. *Guide to Affordable Gemology.* Poulsbo, WA: Hanneman Gemological Instruments, 1998.

Hodgkinson, Alan. *Visual Optics: The Hodgkinson Method.* Gemworld Intl. Inc., Northbrook, IL, 1995.

Hughes, Richard W. *Ruby & Sapphire.* Boulder, CO: RWH Publishing, 1997.

Joseph, Ralph. *Jeweler's Guide to Effective Jewelry Appraising.* Northbrook, IL: Gemworld International, Inc, 1996.

Liddicoat, Richard T. *Handbook of Gem Identification.* Santa Monica, CA: GIA, 1993.

Matlins, Antoinette L. & Bonanno, A. C. *Engagement & Wedding Rings.* South Woodstock, VT: Gemstone Press, 1999.

Miller, Anna M. *Gems and Jewelry Appraising.* New York: Van Nostrand Reinhold Company, 1988.

Miller, Anna. *Buyer's Guide to Affordable Antique Jewelry.* New York: Carol Publishing Group, 1993.

Morton, Philip. *Contemporary Jewelry.* New York: Holt, Rinehart, and Winston, 1976.

Nassau, Kurt. *Gems Made by Man*. Santa Monica, CA. Gemological Institute of America, 1980.

Nassau, Kurt. *Gemstone Enhancement*, Second Edition. London: Butterworths, 1994.

O'Donoghue & Joyner Louise. *Identification of Gemstones*. London, Butterworth Heinemann, 2003.

O'Donoghue, Michael. *Synthetic, Imitation & Treated Gemstones*. Oxford: Butterworth-Heinemann, 1997.

Pinton, Diego. *Jewellery Technology*. Milan: Edizioni Gold Sri, 1999.

Preston, William S. *Guides for the Jewelry Industry*. New York: Jewelers Vigilance Committee, Inc., 1986.

Romero, Christie. *Warman's Jewelry: 3rd Edition*. Iola, WI: Krause Publications, 2002.

Schumann, Walter. *Gemstones of the World:* Revised & Expanded Edition. New York: Sterling 1997.

Sprintzen, Alice. *Jewelry: Basic Techniques and Design*. Radnor, PA: Chilton, 1980

SSEF Swiss Gemmological Institute. *Standards & Applications for Diamond Report,, Gemstone Report, Test Report.*.Basel: SSEF Swiss Gemmological Institute, 1998.

Suwa, Yasukazu. *Gemstones: Quality and Value* (English Edition). Santa Monica, CA: Gemological Institute of America & Suwa & Son, 1994.

Suwa, Yasukazu. *Gemstones: Quality and Value Volume 2*. Tokyo: Sekai Bunka-sha, 1998.

Wise, Richard. *Secrets of the Gem Trade*. Lenox: Brunswick House Press. 2003.

Wykoff, Gerald L. *Beyond the Glitter*. Washington DC: Adamas, 1982.

Periodicals & Miscellaneous

Auction Market Resource for Gems & Jewelry. P. O. Box 7683, Rego Park, NY 11374.

Australian Gemmologist. Brisbane: Gemmological Association of Australia

Canadian Gemmologist. North York, Ontario: Canadian Gemmological Assn.

Conwell, Russell. *Acres of Diamonds*. New York: Jove Books, 1988.

Deljanin, Branko & Sherman, Gregory. *Changing the Color of Diamonds: The High Pressure High Temperature Process Explained*. New York: EGL USA, 2000.

Gems and Gemology. Carlsbad, CA: Gemological Institute of America.

The Guide. Northbrook, IL: Gemworld International Inc. 1999 & 2000.

Jewelers Circular Keystone. Radnor, PA: Chilton Publishing Co.

Jewelers' Quarterly Magazine. Sonoma, CA.

Journal of Gemmology, London: Gemological Association and Gem Testing Laboratory of Great Britain.

Lapidary Journal. Devon, PA: Lapidary Journal Inc.

Modern Jeweler. Lincolnshire, IL: Vance Publishing Inc.

National Jeweler. New York: Gralla Publications.

New York Diamonds. New York: International Diamond Publications, Ltd.

Professional Jeweler. Philadelphia: Bond Communications.

Rapaport Diamond Report. New York: Rapaport Corp.

Index

Order Form

TITLE	Price Each	Quantity	Total
Diamond Handbook	$18.95		
Gemstone Buying Guide	$19.95		
Ruby, Sapphire & Emerald Buying Guide	$19.95		
Gold & Platinum Jewelry Buying Guide	$19.95		
Pearl Buying Guide	$19.95		
Diamond Ring Buying Guide	$17.95		
Gem & Jewelry Pocket Guide	$11.95		
Osteoporosis from a Patient's Point of Vi\ew: A Consumer Approach to Strong Bones & Good Health by Newman (Available 8/05)	$14.95		
		Book Total	
SALES TAX for California residents only	**(book total x $.0825)**		
SHIPPING: USA: first book $2.00, each additional copy $1.25 Foreign – surface mail: first book $6.00 ea. addl. $4.00 Canada & Mexico - airmail: first book $6.50, ea. addl. $4.00 All other foreign countries - airmail: first book $11.00, ea. addl. $7.00			
TOTAL AMOUNT with tax (if applicable) and shipping (Pay foreign orders with an international money order or a check drawn on a U.S. bank.)		**TOTAL**	

Mail check or money order in U.S. funds

To: International Jewelry Publications
P.O. Box 13384
Los Angeles, CA 90013-0384 USA

Ship to:

Name_____

Address_____

City_____ State or Province_____

Postal or Zip Code_____ Country _____